W9-BWR-408

Chicago Public Library

REFERENCE

Form 178 rev. 11-00

career
ideas
for
teens

in
education
and training

Diane Lindsey Reeves
with Gail Karlitz

Ferguson
An imprint of ☑®Facts On File

Career Ideas for Teens in Education and Training

Ferguson
An imprint of Facts On File, Inc.
132 West 31st Street
New York NY 10001

Library of Congress Cataloging-in-Publication Data

Reeves, Diane Lindsey, 1959–
    Career ideas for teens in education and training / Diane Lindsey Reeves with Gail Karlitz.
        p. cm.
    Includes index.
    ISBN 0-8160-5295-6 (hc: alk. paper)
    1. Teaching—Vocational guidance—Juvenile literature. 2. Training—Vocational guidance—Juvenile literature.
    3. Education—Vocational guidance—Juvenile literature. 4. Teenagers—Life skills guides—Juvenile literature.
    I. Karlitz, Gail.   II. Title.
    LB1775.R417 2004
    370'.23'73—dc22

                                                        2004024220

Ferguson books are available at special discounts when purchased in bulk quantities for businesses, associations, institutions, or sales promotions. Please call our Special Sales Department in New York at (212) 967-8800 or (800) 322-8755.

You can find Ferguson on the World Wide Web at http://www.fergpubco.com

Text design by Joel and Sandy Armstrong
Cover design by Nora Wertz
Illustrations by Matt Wood

Printed in the United States of America

VB PKG 10 9 8 7 6 5 4 3 2 1

This book is printed on acid-free paper.

contents

acknowledgments

A million thanks to the people who took the time to share their career
stories and provide photos for this book:

Mary Belkin
BJ Berquist
Carol Carter
Anna Beth Crabtree
William Howe
Barbara Klipper
Chris Bowser
Roger Lazoff
George Megrue
Robert Roberge
Linda Ilene Slone
Lisa Wright

career ideas for teens

welcome to your future

Q: What's one of the most boring questions adults ask teens?

A: "So . . . what do you want to be when you grow up?"

Well-meaning adults always seem so interested in what you plan to be.

You, on the other hand, are just trying to make it through high school in one piece.

But you may still have a nagging feeling that you really need to find some direction and think about what you want to do with your life.

When it comes to choosing your life's work there's some good news and some bad news. The good news is that, according to the U.S. Bureau of Labor Statistics, you have more than 12,000 different occupations to choose from. With that many options there's got to be something that's just right for you.

Right?

Absolutely.

But . . .

Here comes the bad news.

THERE ARE MORE THAN 12,000 DIFFERENT OCCUPATIONS TO CHOOSE FROM!

How in the world are you ever going to figure out which one is right for you?

We're so glad you asked!

Helping high school students like you make informed choices about their future is what this book (and each of the other titles in the *Career Ideas for Teens* series) is all about. Here you'll encounter 10 tough questions designed to help you answer the biggest one of all: "What in the world am I going to do after I graduate from high school?"

The *Career Ideas for Teens* series enables you to expand your horizons beyond the "doctor, teacher, lawyer" responses common to those new to the career exploration process. The books provide a no-pressure introduction to real jobs that real people do. And they offer a chance to "try on" different career options before committing to a specific college program or career path. Each title in this series is based on one of the 16 career clusters established by the U.S. Department of Education.

And what is a career cluster, you ask? Career clusters are based on a simple and very useful concept. Each cluster consists of all entry-level through professional-level occupations in a broad industry area. All of the jobs and industries in a cluster have many things in common. This organizational structure makes it easier for people like you to get a handle on the big world of work. So instead of rushing headlong into a mind-boggling exploration of the entire universe of career opportunities, you get a chance to tiptoe into smaller, more manageable segments first.

We've used this career cluster concept to organize the *Career Ideas for Teens* series of books. For example, careers related to the arts, communication, and entertainment are organized or "clustered" into the *Career Ideas for Teens in the Arts and Communications* title; a wide variety of health care professions are included in *Career Ideas for Teens in Health Science*; and so on.

Clueless as to what some of these industries are all about? Can't even imagine how something like manufacturing or public administration could possibly relate to you?

No problem.

You're about to find out. Just be prepared to expect the unexpected as you venture out into the world of work. There are some pretty incredible options out there, and some pretty surprising ones too. In fact, it's quite possible that you'll discover that the ideal career for you is one you had never heard of before.

Whatever you do, don't cut yourself short by limiting yourself to just one book in the series. You may find that your initial interests guide you towards the health sciences field—which would, of course, be a good place to start. However, you may discover some new "twists" with a look through the arts and communications book. There you may find a way to blend your medical interests with your exceptional writing and speaking skills by considering becoming a public relations (PR) specialist for a hospital or pharmaceutical company. Or look at the book on education to see about becoming a public health educator or school nurse.

Before you get started, you should know that this book is divided into three sections, each representing an important step toward figuring out what to do with your life.

The first eight titles in the *Career Ideas for Teens* series focus on:

- Architecture and Construction
- Arts and Communications
- Education and Training
- Government and Public Service
- Health Science
- Information Technology
- Law and Public Safety
- Manufacturing

welcome to your future

Before You Get Started

Unlike most books, this one is meant to be actively experienced, rather than merely read. Passive perusal won't cut it. Energetic engagement is what it takes to figure out something as important as the rest of your life.

As we've already mentioned, you'll encounter 10 important questions as you work your way through this book. Following each Big Question is an activity designated with a symbol that looks like this:

Every time you see this symbol, you'll know it's time to invest a little energy in your future by getting out your notebook or binder, a pen or pencil, and doing whatever the instructions direct you to do. If this book is your personal property, you can choose to do the activities right in the book. But you still might want to make copies of your finished products to go in a binder so they are all in one place for easy reference.

When you've completed all the activities, you'll have your own personal **Big Question AnswerBook,** a planning guide representing a straightforward and truly effective process you can use throughout your life to make fully informed career decisions.

discover you at work

This first section focuses on a very important subject: You. It poses four Big Questions that are designed specifically to help you "discover you":

❓ Big Question #1: **who are you?**
❓ Big Question #2: **what are your interests and strengths?**
❓ Big Question #3: **what are your work values?**

Then, using an interest assessment tool developed by the U.S. Department of Labor and implemented with your very vivid imagination, you'll picture yourself doing some of the things that people actually do for their jobs. In other words, you'll start "discovering you at work" by answering the following:

❓ Big Question #4: **what's your work personality?**

Unfortunately, this first step is often a misstep for many people. Or make that a "missed" step. When you talk with the adults in your life about their career choices, you're likely to find that some of them never even considered the idea of choosing a career based on personal preferences and strengths. You're also likely to learn that if they had it to do over again, this step would definitely play a significant role in the choices they would make.

explore your options

There's more than meets the eye when it comes to finding the best career to pursue. There are also countless ways to blend talent or passion in these areas in some rather unexpected and exciting ways. Get ready to find answers to two more Big Questions as you browse through an entire section of career profiles:

? Big Question #5: **do you have the right skills?**
? Big Question #6: **are you on the right path?**

experiment with success

At long last you're ready to give this thing called career planning a trial run. Here's where you'll encounter three Big Questions that will unleash critical decision-making strategies and skills that will serve you well throughout a lifetime of career success.

While you're at it, take some time to sit in on a roundtable discussion with successful professionals representing a very impressive array of careers related to this industry. Many of their experiences will apply to your own life, even if you don't plan to pursue the same careers.

? Big Question #7: **who knows what you need to know?**
? Big Question #8: **how can you find out what a career is really like?**
? Big Question #9: **how do you know when you've made the right choice?**

Then as you begin to pull all your new insights and ideas together, you'll come to one final question:

? Big Question #10: **what's next?**

As you get ready to take the plunge, remember that this is a book about possibilities and potential. You can use it to make the most of your future work!

Here's what you'll need to complete the Big Question AnswerBook:

● A notebook or binder for the completed activities included in all three sections of the book
● An openness to new ideas
● Complete and completely candid answers to the 10 Big Question activities

So don't just read it, do it.
Plan it.
Dream it.

discover you at work

The goal here is to get some clues about who you are and what you should do with your life.

As time goes by, you will grow older, become more educated, and have more experiences, but many things that truly define you are not likely to change. Even now you possess very strong characteristics —genuine qualities that mark you as the unique and gifted person that you undoubtedly are.

It's impossible to overestimate the importance of giving your wholehearted attention to this step. You, after all, are the most valuable commodity you'll ever have to offer a future employer. Finding work that makes the most of your assets often means the difference between enjoying a rewarding career and simply earning a paycheck.

You've probably already experienced the satisfaction of a good day's work. You know what we mean—those days when you get all your assignments in on time, you're prepared for the pop quiz your teacher sprung on you, and you beat your best time during sports practice. You may be exhausted at the end of the day but you can't help but feel good about yourself and your accomplishments. A well-chosen career can provide that same sense of satisfaction. Since you're likely to spend upwards of 40 years doing some kind of work, well-informed choices make a lot of sense!

Let's take a little time for you to understand yourself and connect what you discover about yourself to the world of work.

To find a career path that's right for you, we'll tackle these three Big Questions first:

- **who are you?**
- **what are your interests and strengths?**
- **what are your work values?**

Big Question #1:
who are you?

Have you ever noticed how quickly new students in your school or new families in your community find the people who are most like them? If you've ever been the "new" person yourself, you've probably spent your first few days sizing up the general population and then getting in with the people who dress in clothes a lot like yours, appreciate the same style of music, or maybe even root for the same sports teams.

Given that this process happens so naturally—if not necessarily on purpose—it should come as no surprise that many people lean toward jobs that surround them with people most like them. When people with common interests, common values, and complementary talents come together in the workplace, the results can be quite remarkable.

Many career aptitude tests, including the one developed by the U.S. Department of Labor and included later in this book, are based on the theory that certain types of people do better at certain types of jobs. It's like a really sophisticated matchmaking service. Take your basic strengths and interests and match them to the strengths and interests required by specific occupations.

It makes sense when you think about it. When you want to find a career that's ideally suited for you, find out what people like you are doing and head off in that direction!

There's just one little catch.

The only way to recognize other people like you is to recognize yourself. Who are you anyway? What are you like? What's your basic approach to life and work?

Now's as good a time as any to find out. Let's start by looking at who you are in a systematic way. This process will ultimately help you understand how to identify personally appropriate career options.

Big Activity #1:
who are you?

On a sheet of paper, if this book doesn't belong to you, create a list of adjectives that best describe you. You should be able to come up with at least 15 qualities that apply to you. There's no need to make judgments about whether these qualities are good or bad. They just are. They represent who you are and can help you understand what you bring to the workforce.

(If you get stuck, ask a trusted friend or adult to help describe especially strong traits they see in you.)

Some of the types of qualities you may choose to include are:

- **How you relate to others:**
  Are you shy? Outgoing? Helpful? Dependent? Empathic? In charge? Agreeable? Challenging? Persuasive? Popular? Impatient? A loner?
- **How you approach new situations:**
  Are you adventurous? Traditional? Cautious? Enthusiastic? Curious?
- **How you feel about change—planned or unplanned:**
  Are you resistant? Adaptable? Flexible? Predictable?
- **How you approach problems:**
  Are you persistent? Spontaneous? Methodical? Creative?
- **How you make decisions:**
  Are you intuitive? Logical? Emotional? Practical? Systematic? Analytical?
- **How you approach life:**
  Are you laid back? Ambitious? Perfectionist? Idealistic? Optimistic? Pessimistic? Self-sufficient?

Feel free to use any of these words if they happen to describe you well, but please don't limit yourself to this list. Pick the best adjectives that paint an accurate picture of the real you. Get more ideas from a dictionary or thesaurus if you'd like.

When you're finished, put the completed list in your Big Question AnswerBook.

Big Activity #1: who are you?

fifteen qualities that describe me

1

2

3

4

5

6

7

8

9

10

11

12

13

14

15

etc.

Big Question #2:
what are your interests and strengths?

For many people, doing something they like to do is the most important part of deciding on a career path—even more important than how much money they can earn!

We don't all like to do the same things—and that's good. For some people, the ideal vacation is lying on a beach, doing absolutely nothing; others would love to spend weeks visiting museums and historic places. Some people wish they had time to learn to skydive or fly a plane; others like to learn to cook gourmet meals or do advanced math.

If we all liked the same things, the world just wouldn't work very well. There would be incredible crowds in some places and ghost towns in others. Some of our natural resources would be overburdened; others would never be used. We would all want to eat at the same restaurant, wear the same outfit, see the same movie, and live in the same place. How boring!

So let's get down to figuring out what you most like to do and how you can spend your working life doing just that. In some ways your answer to this question is all you really need to know about choosing a career, because the people who enjoy their work the most are those who do something they enjoy. We're not talking rocket science here. Just plain old common sense.

Big Activity # 2:
what are your interests and strengths?

Imagine this: No school, no job, no homework, no chores, no obligations at all. All the time in the world you want to do all the things you like most. You know what we're talking about—those things that completely grab your interest and keep you engrossed for hours without your getting bored. Those kinds of things you do really well—sometimes effortlessly, sometimes with extraordinary (and practiced) skill.

And, by the way, EVERYONE has plenty of both interests and strengths. Some are just more visible than others.

Step 1: Write the three things you most enjoy doing on a sheet of paper, if this book doesn't belong to you. Leave lots of space after each thing.

Step 2: Think about some of the deeper reasons why you enjoy each of these activities—the motivations beyond "it's fun." Do you enjoy shopping because it gives you a chance to be with your friends? Because it allows you to find new ways to express your individuality? Because you enjoy the challenge of finding bargains or things no one else has discovered? Or because it's fun to imagine the lifestyle you'll be able to lead when you're finally rich and famous? In the blank spaces, record the reasons why you enjoy each activity.

Step 3: Keep this list handy in your Big Question AnswerBook so that you can refer to it any time you have to make a vocational decision. Sure, you may have to update the list from time to time as your interests change. But one thing is certain. The kind of work you'll most enjoy will be linked in some way to the activities on that list. Count on it.

Maybe one of your favorite things to do is "play basketball." Does that mean the only way you'll ever be happy at work is to play professional basketball?

Maybe.

Maybe not.

Use your *why* responses to read between the lines. The *why*s can prove even more important than the *what*s. Perhaps what you like most about playing basketball is the challenge or the chance to be part of a team that shares a common goal. Maybe you really like pushing yourself to improve. Or it could be the rush associated with competition and the thrill of winning.

The more you uncover your own *why*s, the closer you'll be to discovering important clues about the kinds of work that are best for you.

Big Activity #2: **what are your interests and strengths?**

things you enjoy doing	why you enjoy doing them
1	• • •
2	• • •
3	• • •

Big Question #3: what are your work values?

Chances are, you've never given a moment's thought to this next question. At least not in the context of career planning.

You already looked at who you are and what you enjoy and do well. The idea being, of course, to seek out career options that make the most of your innate qualities, preferences, and natural abilities.

As you start checking into various careers, you'll discover one more dimension associated with making personally appropriate career choices. You'll find that even though people may have the exact same job title, they may execute their jobs in dramatically different ways. For instance, everyone knows about teachers. They teach things to other people. Period.

But wait. If you line up 10 aspiring teachers in one room, you may be surprised to discover how vastly different their interpretations of the job may be. There are the obvious differences, of course. One may want to teach young children; one may want to teach adults. One will focus on teaching math, while another one focuses on teaching Spanish.

Look a little closer and you'll find even greater disparity in the choices they make. One may opt for the prestige (and paycheck) of working in an Ivy League college, while another is completely committed to teaching disadvantaged children in a remote area of the Appalachian Mountains. One may approach teaching simply as a way to make a living, while another devotes almost every waking hour to working with his or her students.

These subtle but significant differences reflect what's truly important to each person. In a word, they reflect the person's values—those things that are most important to them.

People's values depend on many factors—their upbringing, their life experiences, their goals and ambitions, their religious beliefs, and, quite frankly, the way they view the world and their role in it. Very few people share exactly the same values. However, that doesn't necessarily mean that some people are right and others are wrong. It just means they have different perspectives.

Here's a story that shows how different values can be reflected in career choices.

Imagine: It's five years after college graduation and a group of college friends are back together for the first time. They catch up about their lives, their families, and their careers. Listen in on one of their reunion conversations and see if you can guess what each is doing now.

Alice: I have the best career. Every day I get the chance to help kids with special needs get a good education.

Bob: I love my career, too. It's great to know that I am making my town a safer place for everyone.

Cathy: It was tough for me to commit to more school after college. But I'm glad I did. After all I went through when my parents divorced, I'm glad I can be there to make things easier for other families.

David: I know how you feel. I'm glad I get to do something that helps companies function smoothly and keep our economy strong. Of course, you remember that I had a hard time deciding whether to pursue this career or teaching! This way I get the best of both worlds.

Elizabeth: It's great that we both ended up in the corporate world. You know that I was always intrigued by the stock market.

So exactly what is each of the five former freshman friends doing today? Have you made your guesses?

Alice is a lawyer. She specializes in education law. She makes sure that school districts provide special needs children with all of the resources they are entitled to under the law.

Bob is a lawyer. He is a prosecuting attorney and makes his town safer by ensuring that justice is served when someone commits a crime.

Cathy is a lawyer. She practices family law. She helps families negotiate separation and divorce agreements and makes sure that adoption and custody proceedings protect everyone involved. Sometimes she even provides legal intervention to protect adults or children who are in abusive situations.

David is a lawyer. He practices employment law. He helps companies set up policies that follow fair employment practices. He also gives seminars to managers, teaching them what the law says and means about sexual harassment, discrimination, and termination of employment.

Elizabeth is a lawyer. She practices corporate law and is indispensable to corporations with legal responsibilities towards stockholders and the government.

Wow! All five friends have the same job title. But each describes his/her job so differently! All five were able to enter the field of law and focus on the things that are most important to them: quality education, freedom from crime, protection of families and children, fairness in the workplace, and corporate economic growth. Identifying and honoring your personal values is an important part of choosing your life's work.

Big Activity #3:
what are your work values?

Step 1: Look at the following chart. If this book doesn't belong to you, divide a sheet of paper into the following three columns:

- **Essential**

Statements that fall into this column are very important to you. If the job doesn't satisfy these needs, you're not interested.

- **Okay**

Great if the job satisfies these needs, but you can also live without them.

- **No Way**

Statements that fall into this column represent needs that are not at all important to you or things you'd rather do without or simply couldn't tolerate.

Step 2: Look over the following list of statements representing different work values. Rewrite each statement in the appropriate column. Does the first statement represent something that is critical to you to have in your work? If so, write it in the first column. No big deal either way? Write it in the second column. Couldn't stand it? Write it in the third column. Repeat the same process for each of the value statements.

Step 3: When you're finished, place your complete work values chart in your Big Question AnswerBook.

Got it? Then get with it.

Really think about these issues. Lay it on the line. What values are so deeply ingrained in you that you'd be absolutely miserable if you had to sacrifice them for a job? Religious beliefs and political leanings fall into this category for some people.

Which ones provide room for some give and take? Things like vacation and benefits, working hours, and other issues along those lines may be completely negotiable for some people, but absolutely not for others.

Just remember, wherever you go and whatever you do, be sure that the choices you make are true to you.

Big Activity #3: **what are your work values?**

work values	essential	okay	no way
1. I can count on plenty of opportunity for advancement and taking on more responsibility.			
2. I can work to my fullest potential using all of my abilities.			
3. I would be able to give directions and instructions to others.			
4. I would always know exactly what my manager expects of me.			
5. I could structure my own day.			
6. I would be very busy all day.			
7. I would work in attractive and pleasant surroundings.			
8. My coworkers would be people I might choose as friends.			
9. I would get frequent feedback about my performance.			
10. I could continue my education to progress to an even higher level job.			
11. Most of the time I would be able to work alone.			
12. I would know precisely what I need to do to succeed at the job.			
13. I could make decisions on my own.			

Big Activity #3: **what are your work values?**

work values	essential	okay	no way
14. I would have more than the usual amount of vacation time.			
15. I would be working doing something I really believe in.			
16. I would feel like part of a team.			
17. I would find good job security and stable employment opportunities in the industry.			
18. I could depend on my manager for the training I need.			
19. I would earn lots of money.			
20. I would feel a sense of accomplishment in my work.			
21. I would be helping other people.			
22. I could try out my own ideas.			
23. I would not need to have further training or education to do this job.			
24. I would get to travel a lot.			
25. I could work the kind of hours I need to balance work, family, and personal responsibilities.			

To summarize in my own words, the work values most important to me include:

Big Question #4:
what is
your work
personality?

Congratulations. After completing the first three activities, you've already discovered a set of skills you can use throughout your life. Basing key career decisions on factors associated with who you are, what you enjoy and do well, and what's most important about work will help you today as you're just beginning to explore the possibilities, as well as into the future as you look for ways to cultivate your career.

Now that you've got that mastered, let's move on to another important skill. This one blends some of what you just learned about yourself with what you need to learn about the real world of work. It's a reality check of sorts as you align and merge your personal interests and abilities with those required in different work situations. At the end of this task you will identify your personal interest profile.

This activity is based on the work of Dr. John Holland. Dr. Holland conducted groundbreaking research that identified different characteristics in people. He found that he could classify people into six basic groups based on which characteristics tended to occur at the same time. He also found that the characteristics that defined the different groups of people were also characteristics that corresponded to success in different groups of occupations. The result of all that work was a classification system that identifies and names six distinct groups of people who share personal interests or characteristics and are likely to be successful in a group of clearly identified jobs.

Dr. Holland's work is respected by workforce professionals everywhere and is widely used by employers and employment agencies to help people get a handle on the best types of work to pursue.

The following Work Interest Profiler (WIP) is based on Dr. Holland's theories and was developed by the U.S. Department of Labor's Employment and Training Administration as part of an important project called O*Net. O*Net is a system used in all 50 states to provide career and employment services to thousands of people every year. It's a system you'll want to know about when it's time to take that first plunge into the world of work. If you'd like, you can find more information about this system at ***http://online.onetcenter.org***.

Big Activity #4:
what is your work personality?

By completing O*Net's Work Interest Profiler (WIP), you'll gain valuable insight into the types of work that are right for you.

here's how it works

The WIP lists many activities that real people do at real jobs. Your task is to read a brief statement about each of these activities and decide if it is something you think you'd enjoy doing. Piece of cake!

Don't worry about whether you have enough education or training to perform the activity. And, for now, forget about how much money you would make performing the activity.

Just boil it down to whether or not you'd like performing each work activity. If you'd like it, put a check in the *like* column that corresponds to each of the six interest areas featured in the test on the handy dandy chart you're about to create (or use the one in the book if it's yours). If you don't like it, put that check in the *dislike* column. What if you don't have a strong opinion on a particular activity? That's okay. Count that one as *unsure*.

Be completely honest with yourself. No one else is going to see your chart. If you check things you think you "should" check, you are not helping yourself find the career that will make you happy.

Before you start, create a chart for yourself. Your scoring sheet will have six horizontal rows and three vertical columns. Label the six rows as Sections 1 through 6, and label the three columns *like*, *dislike*, and *unsure*.

how to complete the Work Interest Profiler

Step 1: Start with Section 1.

Step 2: Look at the first activity and decide whether you would like to do it as part of your job.

Step 3: Put a mark in the appropriate column (*Like*, *Dislike*, or *Unsure*) on the Section 1 row.

Step 4: Continue for every activity in Section 1. Then do Sections 2 through 6.

Step 5: When you've finished all of the sections, count the number of marks you have in each column and write down the total.

Remember, this is not a test! There are no right or wrong answers. You are completing this profile to learn more about yourself and your work-related interests.

Also, once you've completed this activity, be sure to put your chart and any notes in your Big Question AnswerBook.

Ready? Let's go!

Section 1

1. Drive a taxi
2. Repair household appliances
3. Catch fish as a member of a fishing crew
4. Paint houses
5. Assemble products in a factory
6. Install flooring in houses
7. Perform lawn care services
8. Drive a truck to deliver packages to homes and offices
9. Work on an offshore oil-drilling rig
10. Put out forest fires
11. Fix a broken faucet
12. Refinish furniture
13. Guard money in an armored car
14. Lay brick or tile
15. Operate a dairy farm
16. Raise fish in a fish hatchery
17. Build a brick walkway
18. Enforce fish and game laws
19. Assemble electronic parts
20. Build kitchen cabinets
21. Maintain the grounds of a park
22. Operate a motorboat to carry passengers
23. Set up and operate machines to make products
24. Spray trees to prevent the spread of harmful insects
25. Monitor a machine on an assembly line

Section 2

1. Study space travel
2. Develop a new medicine
3. Study the history of past civilizations
4. Develop a way to better predict the weather
5. Determine the infection rate of a new disease
6. Study the personalities of world leaders
7. Investigate the cause of a fire
8. Develop psychological profiles of criminals
9. Study whales and other types of marine life
10. Examine blood samples using a microscope
11. Invent a replacement for sugar
12. Study genetics
13. Do research on plants or animals
14. Study weather conditions
15. Investigate crimes
16. Study ways to reduce water pollution
17. Develop a new medical treatment or procedure
18. Diagnose and treat sick animals
19. Conduct chemical experiments
20. Study rocks and minerals
21. Do laboratory tests to identify diseases
22. Study the structure of the human body
23. Plan a research study
24. Study the population growth of a city
25. Make a map of the bottom of the ocean

Section 3

1. Paint sets for a play
2. Create special effects for movies
3. Write reviews of books or movies
4. Compose or arrange music
5. Design artwork for magazines
6. Pose for a photographer
7. Create dance routines for a show
8. Play a musical instrument
9. Edit movies
10. Sing professionally
11. Announce a radio show
12. Perform stunts for a movie or television show
13. Design sets for plays
14. Act in a play
15. Write a song
16. Perform jazz or tap dance
17. Sing in a band
18. Direct a movie
19. Write scripts for movies or television shows
20. Audition singers and musicians for a musical show
21. Conduct a musical choir
22. Perform comedy routines in front of an audience
23. Dance in a Broadway show
24. Perform as an extra in movies, plays, or television shows
25. Write books or plays

Section 4

1. Teach children how to play sports
2. Help people with family-related problems
3. Teach an individual an exercise routine
4. Perform nursing duties in a hospital
5. Help people with personal or emotional problems
6. Teach work and living skills to people with disabilities
7. Assist doctors in treating patients
8. Work with juveniles on probation
9. Supervise the activities of children at a camp
10. Teach an elementary school class
11. Perform rehabilitation therapy
12. Help elderly people with their daily activities
13. Help people who have problems with drugs or alcohol
14. Teach a high school class
15. Give career guidance to people
16. Do volunteer work at a non-profit organization
17. Help families care for ill relatives
18. Teach sign language to people with hearing disabilities
19. Help people with disabilities improve their daily living skills
20. Help conduct a group therapy session
21. Work with children with mental disabilities
22. Give CPR to someone who has stopped breathing
23. Provide massage therapy to people
24. Plan exercises for patients with disabilities
25. Counsel people who have a life-threatening illness

Section 5

1. Sell CDs and tapes at a music store
2. Manage a clothing store
3. Sell houses
4. Sell computer equipment in a store
5. Operate a beauty salon or barber shop
6. Sell automobiles
7. Represent a client in a lawsuit
8. Negotiate business contracts
9. Sell a soft drink product line to stores and restaurants
10. Start your own business
11. Be responsible for the operations of a company
12. Give a presentation about a product you are selling
13. Buy and sell land
14. Sell restaurant franchises to individuals
15. Manage the operations of a hotel
16. Negotiate contracts for professional athletes
17. Sell merchandise at a department store
18. Market a new line of clothing
19. Buy and sell stocks and bonds
20. Sell merchandise over the telephone
21. Run a toy store
22. Sell hair-care products to stores and salons
23. Sell refreshments at a movie theater
24. Manage a retail store
25. Sell telephone and other communication equipment

Section 6

1. Develop an office filing system
2. Generate the monthly payroll checks for an office
3. Proofread records or forms
4. Schedule business conferences
5. Enter information into a database
6. Photocopy letters and reports
7. Keep inventory records
8. Record information from customers applying for charge accounts
9. Load computer software into a large computer network
10. Use a computer program to generate customer bills
11. Develop a spreadsheet using computer software
12. Operate a calculator
13. Direct or transfer office phone calls
14. Use a word processor to edit and format documents
15. Transfer funds between banks, using a computer
16. Compute and record statistical and other numerical data
17. Stamp, sort, and distribute office mail
18. Maintain employee records
19. Record rent payments
20. Keep shipping and receiving records
21. Keep accounts payable/receivable for an office
22. Type labels for envelopes and packages
23. Calculate the wages of employees
24. Take notes during a meeting
25. Keep financial records

Section 1
Realistic

	Like	Dislike	Unsure
1.			
2.			
3.			
4.			
5.			
6.			
7.			
8.			
9.			
10.			
11.			
12.			
13.			
14.			
15.			
16.			
17.			
18.			
19.			
20.			
21.			
22.			
23.			
24.			
25.			

Total Realistic

Section 2
Investigative

	Like	Dislike	Unsure
1.			
2.			
3.			
4.			
5.			
6.			
7.			
8.			
9.			
10.			
11.			
12.			
13.			
14.			
15.			
16.			
17.			
18.			
19.			
20.			
21.			
22.			
23.			
24.			
25.			

Total Investigative

Section 3
Artistic

	Like	Dislike	Unsure
1.			
2.			
3.			
4.			
5.			
6.			
7.			
8.			
9.			
10.			
11.			
12.			
13.			
14.			
15.			
16.			
17.			
18.			
19.			
20.			
21.			
22.			
23.			
24.			
25.			

Total Artistic

Section 4
Social

	Like	Dislike	Unsure
1.			
2.			
3.			
4.			
5.			
6.			
7.			
8.			
9.			
10.			
11.			
12.			
13.			
14.			
15.			
16.			
17.			
18.			
19.			
20.			
21.			
22.			
23.			
24.			
25.			

Total Social

Section 5
Enterprising

	Like	Dislike	Unsure
1.			
2.			
3.			
4.			
5.			
6.			
7.			
8.			
9.			
10.			
11.			
12.			
13.			
14.			
15.			
16.			
17.			
18.			
19.			
20.			
21.			
22.			
23.			
24.			
25.			

Total Enterprising

Section 6
Conventional

	Like	Dislike	Unsure
1.			
2.			
3.			
4.			
5.			
6.			
7.			
8.			
9.			
10.			
11.			
12.			
13.			
14.			
15.			
16.			
17.			
18.			
19.			
20.			
21.			
22.			
23.			
24.			
25.			

Total Conventional

What are your top three work personalities? List them here if this is your own book or on a separate piece of paper if it's not.

1. _____
2. _____
3. _____

all done? let's see what it means

Be sure you count up the number of marks in each column on your scoring sheet and write down the total for each column. You will probably notice that you have a lot of *likes* for some sections, and a lot of *dislikes* for other sections. The section that has the most *likes* is your primary interest area. The section with the next highest number of *likes* is your second interest area. The next highest is your third interest area.

Now that you know your top three interest areas, what does it mean about your work personality type? We'll get to that in a minute, but first we are going to answer a couple of other questions that might have crossed your mind:

- What is the best work personality to have?
- What does my work personality mean?

First of all, there is no "best" personality in general. There is, however, a "best" personality for each of us. It's who we really are and how we feel most comfortable. There may be several "best" work personalities for any job because different people may approach the job in different ways. But there is no "best work personality."

Asking about the "best work personality" is like asking whether the "best" vehicle is a sports car, a sedan, a station wagon, or a sports utility vehicle. It all depends on who you are and what you need.

One thing we do know is that our society needs all of the work personalities in order to function effectively. Fortunately, we usually seem to have a good mix of each type.

So, while many people may find science totally boring, there are many other people who find it fun and exciting. Those are the people who invent new technologies, who become doctors and researchers, and who turn natural resources into the things we use every day. Many people may think that spending a day with young children is unbearable, but those who love that environment are the teachers, community leaders, and museum workers that nurture children's minds and personalities.

When everything is in balance, there's a job for every person and a person for every job.

Now we'll get to your work personality. Following are descriptions of each of Dr. Holland's six work personalities that correspond to the six sections in your last exercise. You, like most people, are a unique combination of more than one. A little of this, a lot of that. That's what makes us interesting.

Identify your top three work personalities. Also, pull out your responses to the first three exercises we did. As you read about your top three work personalities, see how they are similar to the way you described yourself earlier.

Type 1
Realistic

Realistic people are often seen as the "Doers." They have mechanical or athletic ability and enjoy working outdoors.

Realistic people like work activities that include practical, hands-on problems and solutions. They enjoy dealing with plants, animals, and real-life materials like wood, tools, and machinery.

Careers that involve a lot of paperwork or working closely with others are usually not attractive to realistic people.

Who you are:
independent
reserved
practical
mechanical
athletic
persistent

What you like to do/what you do well:
build things
train animals
play a sport
fix things
garden
hunt or fish
woodworking

repair cars
refinish furniture

Career possibilities:
aerospace engineer
aircraft pilot
animal breeder
architect
baker/chef
building inspector
carpenter
chemical engineer
civil engineer
construction manager
dental assistant
detective
glazier
jeweler
machinist
oceanographer
optician
park ranger
plumber
police officer
practical nurse
private investigator
radiologist
sculptor

Type 2
Investigative

Investigative people are often seen as the "Thinkers." They much prefer searching for facts and figuring out problems mentally to doing physical activity or leading other people.

If Investigative is one of your strong interest areas, your answers to the earlier exercises probably matched some of these:

Who you are:
curious
logical
independent
analytical
observant
inquisitive

What you like to do/what you do well:
think abstractly
solve problems
use a microscope
do research
fly a plane
explore new subjects
study astronomy
do puzzles
work with a computer

Career possibilities:

aerospace engineer
archaeologist
CAD technician
chemist
chiropractor
computer programmer
coroner
dentist
electrician
ecologist
geneticist
hazardous waste technician
historian
horticulturist
management consultant
medical technologist
meteorologist
nurse practitioner
pediatrician
pharmacist
political scientist
psychologist
software engineer
surgeon
technical writer
veterinarian
zoologist

Type 3
Artistic

Artistic people are the "Creators." People with this primary interest like work activities that deal with the artistic side of things.

Artistic people need to have the opportunity for self-expression in their work. They want to be able to use their imaginations and prefer to work in less structured environments, without clear sets of rules about how things should be done.

Who you are:

imaginative
intuitive
expressive
emotional
creative
independent

What you like to do/what you do well:

draw
paint
play an instrument
visit museums
act
design clothes or rooms
read fiction
travel
write stories, poetry, or music

Career possibilities:

architect
actor
animator
art director
cartoonist
choreographer
costume designer
composer
copywriter
dancer
disc jockey
drama teacher
emcee
fashion designer
graphic designer
illustrator
interior designer
journalist
landscape architect
medical illustrator
photographer
producer
scriptwriter
set designer

Type 4
Social

Social people are known as the "Helpers." They are interested in work that can assist others and promote learning and personal development.

Communication with other people is very important to those in the Social group. They usually do not enjoy jobs that require a great amount of work with objects, machines, or data. Social people like to teach, give advice, help, cure, or otherwise be of service to people.

Who you are:
friendly
outgoing
empathic
persuasive
idealistic
generous

What you like to do/what you do well:
teach others
work in groups
play team sports
care for children
go to parties
help or advise others
meet new people

express yourself
join clubs or organizations

Career possibilities:
animal trainer
arbitrator
art teacher
art therapist
audiologist
child care worker
clergy person
coach
counselor/therapist
cruise director
dental hygienist
employment interviewer
EMT worker
fitness trainer
flight attendant
occupational therapist
police officer
recreational therapist
registered nurse
school psychologist
social worker
substance abuse counselor
teacher
tour guide

Type 5
Enterprising

Enterprising work personalities can be called the "Persuaders." These people like work activities that have to do with starting up and carrying out projects, especially business ventures. They like taking risks for profit, enjoy being responsible for making decisions, and generally prefer action to thought or analysis.

People in the Enterprising group like to work with other people. While the Social group focuses on helping other people, members of the Enterprising group are able to lead, manage, or persuade other people to accomplish the goals of the organization.

Who you are:
assertive
self-confident
ambitious
extroverted
optimistic
adventurous

What you like to do/what you do well:
organize activities
sell things
promote ideas

discuss politics
hold office in clubs
give talks or speeches
meet people
initiate projects
start your own business

Career possibilities:
advertising
chef
coach, scout
criminal investigator
economist
editor
foreign service officer
funeral director
hotel manager
journalist
lawyer
lobbyist
public relations specialist
newscaster
restaurant manager
sales manager
school principal
ship's captain
stockbroker
umpire, referee
urban planner

Type 6
Conventional

People in the Conventional group are the "Organizers." They like work activities that follow set procedures and routines. They are more comfortable and proficient working with data and detail than they are with generalized ideas.

Conventional people are happiest in work situations where the lines of authority are clear, where they know exactly what responsibilities are expected of them, and where there are precise standards for the work.

Who you are:
well-organized
accurate
practical
persistent
conscientious
ambitious

What you like to do/what you do well:
work with numbers
type accurately
collect or organize things
follow up on tasks
be punctual
be responsible for details
proofread

keep accurate records
understand regulations

Career possibilities:
accountant
actuary
air traffic controller
assessor
budget analyst
building inspector
chief financial officer
corporate treasurer
cost estimator
court reporter
economist
environmental compliance lawyer
fire inspector
insurance underwriter
legal secretary
mathematician
medical secretary
proofreader
tax preparer

education and training careers
work personality chart

Once you've discovered your own unique work personality code, you can use it to explore the careers profiled in this book and elsewhere. Do keep in mind though that this code is just a tool meant to help focus your search. It's not meant to box you in or to keep you from pursuing any career that happens to capture your imagination.

Following is a chart listing the work personality codes associated with each of the careers profiled in this book

	Realistic	Investigative	Artistic	Social	Enterprising	Conventional
My Work Personality Code (mark your top three areas)						
Animal Trainer	X			X	X	
Audiologist	X	X		X		
Career and Technical Education Instructor				X	X	X
Career Counselor			X	X	X	
Coach	X			X	X	
College Professor			X	X	X	
Cooperative Extension Agent	X			X	X	
Corporate Trainer				X	X	X
Correctional Educator			X	X	X	
Education Attorney			X	X	X	
Elementary School Teacher			X	X	X	
English as a Second Language (ESL) Instructor			X	X		X
Environmental Educator	X			X	X	
Fitness Trainer	X			X	X	
Guidance Counselor				X	X	X
Instructional Coordinator	X			X	X	
Librarian	X			X		X

	Realistic	Investigative	Artistic	Social	Enterprising	Conventional
My Work Personality Code (mark your top three areas)						
Library Technician	X			X		X
Museum Educator	X			X	X	
Paraprofessional				X	X	X
Physical Education Teacher	X			X	X	
Preschool Teacher			X	X	X	
Principal		X		X	X	
Public Health Educator			X	X	X	
School Media Specialist	X			X		X
School Nurse		X		X	X	
School Psychologist		X	X	X		
School Social Worker			X	X	X	
Secondary School Teacher			X	X	X	
Service Animal Instructor	X			X	X	
Special Education Teacher				X	X	X
Speech-Language Pathologist		X	X	X		
Student Affairs Officer		X			X	X
Studio Animal Trainer	X			X	X	
Teacher of the Visually Impaired				X	X	X

Now it's time to move on to the next big step in the Big Question process. While the first step focused on you, the next one focuses on the world of work. It includes profiles of a wide variety of occupations related to education and training, a roundtable discussion with professionals working in these fields, and a mind-boggling list of other careers to consider when wanting to blend passion or talent in these areas with your life's work.

SECTION 2 explore your options

By now you probably have a fairly good understanding of the assets (some fully realized and perhaps others only partially developed) that you bring to your future career. You've defined your key characteristics, identified special interests and strengths, examined your work values, and analyzed your basic work personality traits. All in all, you've taken a good, hard look at yourself and we're hoping that you're encouraged by all the potential you've discovered.

Now it's time to look at the world of work.

For careers in education and training, the workplace includes child care centers, schools, colleges and universities, corporate offices, and other places where teaching and learning occur on a regular basis.

The success of every industry and profession you can imagine hinges on the success of education and training. Think about it. Without educators and trainers there would be no doctors, no engineers, no lawyers. Without the efforts of educators and trainers workers in every profession would lack even the basic skills necessary to read, write, and function in civilized society.

When you think of careers in education and training, the first idea that pops into your head is probably "teacher." And, of course, teachers are a big part of the education and training "industry." However, meeting the needs of millions of learners every year requires the services of a wide variety of professionals who plan, manage, and provide actual education and training services as well as the support services that make learning possible.

fyi Each of the following profiles includes several common elements to help guide you through an effective career exploration process. For each career, you'll find:

- A sidebar loaded with information you can use to find out more about the profession. Professional associations, pertinent reading materials, the lowdown on wages and suggested training requirements, and a list of typical types of employers are all included to give you a broader view of what the career is all about.
- An informative essay describing what the career involves.
- Get Started Now strategies you can use right now to get prepared, test the waters, and develop your skills.
  - A Hire Yourself project providing realistic activities like those you would actually find on the job. Try these learning activities and find out what it's really like to be a . . . you name it.

You don't have to read the profiles in order. You may want to first browse through the career ideas that appear to be most interesting. Then check out the others—you never know what might interest you when you know more about it. As you read each profile, think about how well it matches up with what you learned about yourself in: **discover you at work**. Narrow down your options to a few careers and use the rating system described below to evaluate your interest levels.

- **No way!** There's not even a remote chance that this career is a good fit for me. (Since half of figuring out what you do want to do in life involves figuring out what you don't want to do, this is not a bad place to be.)
- **This is intriguing.** I want to learn more about it and look at similar careers as well. (The activities outlined in: **experiment with success** will be especially useful in this regard.)
- **This is it!** It's the career I've been looking for all my life and I want to go after it with all I've got. (Head straight to: **experiment with success.**)

In the following section, you'll find in-depth profiles of 35 careers related in one way or another to education. As you explore these (and other) careers, you may notice that some careers are more alike than others. The careers that have a lot in common can be grouped into different "pathways." Understanding these pathways provides another important clue about which direction might be best for you. The three education and training pathways include:

Teaching and Training

According to experts associated with the U.S. Department of Education's career cluster initiative, there are excellent opportunities ahead for people who choose to pursue careers in teaching and training. A huge demand is expected for well-educated professionals with the ability to effectively communicate their knowledge in a given subject to people of all ages. Many occupations in this field require licensing or certification in addition to postsecondary credentials that range from the associate's degrees in child development required for many child care workers to the doctorates required for college professors.

Training and education careers profiled in this book include career and technical education instructor, coach, college and university professor, cooperative extension agent, corporate trainer, elementary teacher, English as a second language (ESL) instructor, environmental educator, fitness trainer, museum educator, paraprofessional, physical education teacher, public health educator, secondary school teacher, and special education teacher.

Professional Support Services

The professional support pathway represents a wide variety of highly specialized professions that enhance and sustain the education system. This pathway includes those professions that assist people with personal and family needs, mental health problems, educational goals, and career decision making. Most of the work conducted by these professionals takes place outside of classrooms and their services are often provided to individuals and families as opposed to groups of students.

Careers in this pathway that are profiled in this book include audiologist, career counselor, guidance counselor, school psychologist, and school social worker.

Administration and Administrative Support

Keeping educational programs and facilities running smoothly is the number one priority of administration and administrative support personnel. Administrators provide the direction, leadership, and manage-

A Note on Websites

Websites tend to move around a bit. If you have trouble finding a particular site, use an Internet browser to search for a specific website or type of information.

ment that make for effective learning environments at every level whether it's a preschool, a university, a correctional facility, or a job training organization.

Education attorney and advocate, instructional coordinator, principal, and student affairs officer are examples of administration and administrative support professions that are profiled in this book.

As you explore the individual careers in this book and others in this series, remember to keep what you've learned about yourself in mind. Consider each option in light of what you know about your interests, strengths, work values, and work personality.

Pay close attention to the job requirements. Does it require math aptitude? Good writing skills? Ability to take things apart and visualize how they go back together? If you don't have the necessary abilities (or don't have a strong desire to acquire them), you probably won't enjoy the job.

For instance, enriching young minds may sound like a noble profession and it is. However, when considering whether teaching is right for you, think about the realities of being in a classroom with children or adults all day—every day, week after week, year after year. For some people, this is an exciting and fulfilling prospect. If this is the case for you, be sure to explore every available opportunity to teach or train until you find just the right place to share your skills and expertise.

For those who suspect they might not flourish in a situation involving daily involvement with rooms full of people—young or old—there are other options. If preparing others for productive futures is an important value that you absolutely want to incorporate into your vocation, be open to some of the very interesting options associated with administration or professional support.

animal trainer

Animals definitely enrich our lives. "Working animals," such as the assistance animals trained by service animal instructors, who have their own profile in this book, are trained to perform specialized tasks for people who need them. Pets or companion animals keep us company, entertain us, and protect us. Very well-behaved animals can help children learn to read, raise the spirits of hospital and nursing home residents, and even diagnose diseases for us. Not-so-well-behaved animals can destroy furniture, clothing, and friendships.

Trained animals add an extra dimension to movies, television shows, commercials and stage shows. The trainer's goal is the same for a puppy, an elephant, or anything in between—to modify the animal's behavior, starting with basic obedience. That means the basic "DOs": come when called, walk calmly on a leash, and stay when told to stay; and the basic "DO NOTs": destroy the furniture, bark when there's no emergency, attack visitors, or use the carpet as a bathroom.

Training techniques are basically the same for any animal. These techniques have changed a lot over the years. For a long time, trainers used "punishment reinforcement," beating the animal or striking it with a hot iron whenever it did something that was not what the trainer wanted, but now trainers rely on "positive reinforcement," or rewarding good behavior.

Get Started Now!

- Spend as much time with animals as you can. Volunteer with a veterinarian, shelter, nature center, or zoo.
- Work on oral presentation skills that you will need for training the animal owners or for education programs.
- Curious about how the animals in the movies did their scenes? Check out the American Humane Society Animal Films Updates site at *www.ahafilm.org/reviews.html*.

Search It!
American Kennel Club at *www.AKC.org* and American Association of Zoo Keepers at *www.aazk.org*

Read It!
All about clicker training at *www.clickertrain.com* and at *www.clickersolutions.com/articles/ 2001/ocguide.htm*

Learn It!
- To train domestic pets, learn from another trainer or go to an animal training school
- To train animals for performance, education, or zoos, take classes at a school for animal training

Earn It!
Median annual salary is $27,210. (Source: U.S. Department of Labor)

Find It!
Trainers work for veterinarians, independent training schools, zoos, and agencies that provide animals and trainers to film, television, and commercial production studios.

Hire Yourself!

You've just been hired as a trainer/educator for the new Big Cats exhibit at your local zoo. They want you to prepare a visitor program that includes demonstrations by the animals. Decide what tricks you will have the animals learn. Write out what you will say during their performance that will help visitors understand how these abilities are helpful to the animals in the wild.

No formal schooling is required in order to become an animal trainer, but going through a training program is a really good idea. Such programs give trainers a better understanding of animal learning theory, common behavior problems, and safety training, and can also provide practice working with a professional trainer. Because so much of animal training is training the animal's owner as well as the animal itself, trainers also need to feel comfortable with public speaking and with working in a classroom environment.

What are other reasons to train animals? Trainers who work in zoos or similar environments can use their skills to help educate children and adults about the animals. In modern zoos and aquariums, sometimes called wildlife conservation parks, zookeepers no longer just feed, water, and clean the shelters of their animals, but often work more extensively with the animals as well.

Training the animals, or modifying their behavior, also helps zoos manage them and keep them healthy. When animals are trained to enter chutes or crates in response to trainers' commands and rewards, caretakers are able to take blood or urine samples, give vaccinations, treat wounds, and perform other minor procedures without the need for chemical or physical restraints. Some animals have been trained to open their mouths for exams or present various body parts to the cage mesh, allowing keepers and veterinarians to examine them more frequently and without using restraints.

How do well-behaved animals help to improve people's lives? Programs such as Salt Lake City's Reading Education Assistance Dogs (R.E.A.D., wherein children read to trained therapy animals instead of another person, creating a less intimidating and more helpful and fun environment in which learning is facilitated) have not only improved the reading skills but also the self-esteem and learning attitudes of hundreds of children. Dogs are also being trained to use their incredible sense of smell to sniff out the earliest stages of skin cancer, to identify early lung cancer from breath tests, and to find signatures of prostate cancer in urine samples.

Volunteers who bring their trained animals to schools, hospitals, and hospices have found the patients they visit to be less lonely, less depressed, and easier to talk to. This "animal-assisted therapy" often results in patients having lower blood pressure and improved movement and flexibility as patients stretch and turn to pet the animals. Patients are often reported to be more active and responsive after the visits.

find your future audiologist

audiologist

What does it mean to have a hearing problem? Certain communication limitations are obvious: using telephones, participating in concerts, and attending religious services and other types of public events. Even conducting conversations can be especially challenging. But there are other problems that can have more serious results. For children with undiagnosed and untreated hearing problems, everyday situations such as walking across a street or playing near a hot stove can become especially dangerous due to the inability to hear safety warnings. In school, learning can be compromised or downright impossible when students cannot adequately hear classroom instructions. Similarly, think of the repercussions for hearing impaired adults who cannot respond to a smoke alarm, doorbell, crying baby, or alarm clock.

Hearing loss can occur from genetic causes, exposure to loud noises, illness or infection, injury to the head, exposure to certain drugs, and aging. It is estimated that more than 28 million Americans experience various degrees of hearing loss.

Early detection is the best way to respond to any type of hearing loss. That's why the role of educational audiologists is so important.

Get Started Now!

● Give yourself a virtual tour of the ear at the Augustana College website (*www.augie.edu/perry/ear/ear.htm*). Check out the links to hearing mechanisms, hearing disorders, and audiological rehabilitation.
● Take high school courses in biology, physics, math, and psychology. There are not many undergraduate degrees in audiology so you'll want to consider majoring in communication sciences, psychology, or something similar.
● Take a noncredit course in American Sign Language or lip reading.

Hire Yourself!

Divide a sheet of paper into three columns. In the first column, make a list of some of the everyday challenges faced by people who have hearing loss. Be sure to leave plenty of space for each entry on this list.

Second, come up with a creative solution for each. For example, someone who cannot hear a doorbell might respond to a flashing overhead light. Write a brief description of your idea in the second column.

Third, choose a favorite Internet search engine such as *www.google.com* or *www.yahoo.com* to find information about "assistive technology for the hearing impaired." See how many solutions you find to the problems your list identifies. Write a brief description of a solution or print out a small picture of a device and paste it in the third column of your chart.

According to the Educational Audiology Association (EAA), educational audiologists are audiologists who specialize in the management of hearing and hearing impairment within the educational environment.

Audiologists work with students of all ages to identify hearing loss, balance, and related disorders. At a minimum a school audiologist is responsible for conducting assessment tests and developing treatment plans. Treatment for children may include the use of devices that enhance the child's ability to hear, such as hearing aids or cochlear implants. In some cases, treatment plans may call for learning alternative means of communication, such as sign language or lip reading. In most cases counseling is an important part of the process for both the child and his parents as a means to identify coping strategies and to initiate strategies for preventing further loss of hearing where possible.

Other duties assumed by school audiologists include coordinating school-wide hearing screening programs, conducting comprehensive hearing evaluations with individual students, providing ongoing management for students using hearing aids and other assistive devices, providing parents and school personnel with medical and community referrals, and providing training sessions to school staff. In some cases, school audiologists may also provide therapy in the areas of speech, reading, listening, and hearing aid care.

Educating the public is also part of an educational audiologist's job. Especially important are their outreach efforts toward parents and classroom teachers to enlist them as allies in early detection. But helping children understand how to prevent hearing loss through proper ear care and by avoiding noise pollution is equally important.

In addition to working in school settings, audiologists find opportunities in hospitals, doctor's offices, clinics, research laboratories, and certain types of corporations such as factories and other noise-intensive worksites.

Employment of audiologists is expected to increase much faster than the average for all occupations through the year 2012, primarily due to increasing numbers of baby boomers experiencing hearing problems as they reach the age where problems can be expected to occur. However, employment for school audiologists is also expected to increase as school enrollments grow and as preschoolers are identified as eligible to receive special education services under the reauthorization of the Individuals with Disabilities Education Act (IDEA).

find **career and technical education instructor** your future

career and technical education instructor

According to the Association of Career and Technical Education, "Sixty percent of tomorrow's jobs start with today's career and technical education!" Career and technical education instructors work with young people and adults to prepare them for highly skilled occupations as varied as aircraft pilot, computer programmer, dietician, graphic artist, med-

Get Started Now!

- Find out if your school or school district offers career academies or magnet schools and investigate enrolling in a program that interests you.
- Think about joining career-focused clubs at your school such as Family Career and Community Leaders of America (FCCLA) and DECA, the association for students and teachers of marketing, management and entrepreneurship. Check out their websites for information: *www.fhahero.org* and *www.deca.org*.
- Join your local chapter of SkillsUSA or see if a teacher in your school would be willing to start a new chapter. To find out about SkillsUSA national leadership and skills conference or the SkillsUSA Championships go on-line to *www.skillsusa.org*.
- Use some of your elective credits to take courses related to specific vocations or career paths. Ask your school guidance counselor about opportunities available at your school.

Search It!
Association of Career and Technical Education (ACTE) at *www.acteonline.org*, American Society for Training and Development at *www.astd.org*, and The National Centers for Career and Technical Education at *www.nccte.com*

Read It!
Check out resources at the ACTE website (*www.acteonline.org/professional_development*)

Learn It!
- Bachelor's degree in education or field related to specific career area
- Specialized training in technical trade or experience in industry

Earn It!
Median annual salary is $45,850. (Source: U.S. Department of Labor)

Find It!
Find out about opportunities at the Edweek website at *www.edweek.org/jobs* and *Chronicle of Higher Education* at *www.chronicle.com*.

Hire Yourself!

Your town wants to increase its career and technical education programs. Some parents are hesitant to let their students enroll, thinking that careers that don't require four years of college cannot be interesting, challenging, or financially rewarding. Your job is to create a presentation promoting one of the careers that can result from technical training (such as health care, information technology, or manufacturing). Visit the ACTE website at *www.getcareerskills.com* for ideas. Make sure that you build a case for how exciting and rewarding these careers can be.

ical assistant, nuclear medicine technologist, plumber, veterinary assistant, and welder (to name just a few). Some career and technical educators can work with students in middle school, high school, or college, while others work with adults already out in the workforce.

Career and technical education (CTE) is much more than just learning the skills for a specific job. It also involves presenting traditional academic subject matter (language arts, science, math, and social studies) in ways that link information with skills used in the context of the real world. It also focuses on helping students gain competencies in other job-related skills like responsibility and workplace ethics.

At the middle school level, career and technical education teachers tend to introduce students to opportunities in a wide variety of fields, such as health care, business, auto repair, communications, and technology. Things get more specific at the high school level where work-based activities are often mixed with classroom learning. CTE instructors may teach within a traditional high school, or they may teach in specialty schools such as magnet schools or programs geared to a particular career field. Often, the courses they offer are those that are in especially high demand by area employers who may provide input into the curriculum and offer internships to students. In some cases, students who participate in these programs graduate with certification in a certain program as well as a diploma.

At the post-high school level, these educators work at community colleges or specialized technical schools, providing instruction for occupations that do not require a four-year college degree, such as welder, dental hygienist, X-ray technician, auto mechanic, and cosmetologist. Classes are often taught in real-life settings, so students can become familiar with the environments in which they will ultimately work, and at the same time get practical, hands-on experience. For example, welding instructors show students various welding techniques, watch them use tools and equipment, and have them repeat procedures until they meet the specific standards required by the trade.

At all school levels, career and technical education teachers have many of the same responsibilities as other high school or college teachers: they prepare lessons, grade papers, attend faculty meetings, and keep abreast of developments in their field. They also work closely with the local community and the students' transition from school to work by helping establish internships and by providing information about prospective employers.

When career and technical educators work with adults, they may be training people who are currently unemployed, participating in welfare-to-work programs, or upgrading skills to advance in their careers.

Career and technical education instructors face many of the same challenges as any other high school, college, or adult education teacher, but also face some challenges unique to their area. Like all teachers, they need to understand the content of what they are teaching. In career and technical education, however, it's a lot harder for an instructor to teach a class out of his or her main area of expertise. While it would not be very difficult for an aspiring chemistry teacher to double-major in biology as well, eventually teaching both subjects, it would be far more difficult for a teacher trained in graphic arts to also teach a class for landscapers or nuclear medicine technologists.

An increasing number of employers report growing needs for the well-trained, highly-skilled employees often associated with career and technical education programs. For instance, the National Association of Manufacturers projects a need for 10 million new skilled workers by 2020. Other industries such as construction and public service are predicting similar increased needs. Workforce demographics indicate that there will be a big demand for CTE professionals in coming years.

Search It!
American Counseling Association at *www.counseling.org* and National Career Development Association at *www.ncda.org*

Read It!
Counseling Today Online at *www.counseling.org/ctonline* and Career Convergence at *www.ncda.org*

Learn It!
● Undergraduate degree in psychology, education, social work, or sociology
● Master's degree required for certification to work in some school situations

Earn It!
Median annual salary is $44,100. (Source: U.S. Department of Labor)

Find It!
Search for "career counselor" opportunities using on-line job banks like Monster (*www.monster.com*) and CareerBuilder (*www.careerbuilder.com*).

career counselor

According to research done in 2002 by the Bureau of Labor Statistics (part of the Department of Labor), the average person can expect to change careers five to seven times during his or her work life. People change careers for a variety of reasons. Sometimes the career they selected turns out to be very different from what they expected and not at all what they wanted. Other times, they may eventually conclude that the income, required hours, or the location do not support other priorities in their lives. Some people are forced by other circumstances to change careers. For example, when the dot-com industry fell apart in the 1990s, many people had to find new industries or careers that could use their skills.

A career counselor's primary job is to help people find occupational options that are a good fit for their interests, skills, and goals. This process often starts by guiding clients through a thorough self-assessment process. To do that, career counselors must have excellent skills in listening to their clients and in administering and interpreting assessment tests.

Once a general career focus is determined, career counselors must rely on an excellent knowledge of the world of work to help clients make informed education and employment choices. This knowledge

Get Started Now!
● Visit the career or guidance counselor at your school to find out more about his or her job.
● Enroll in any career exploration courses your school may offer—a smart move whether or not you ever end up becoming a career counselor.
● Learn about trends in employment and how technology and economic factors will cause certain job markets to grow or decline.

Hire Yourself!

It's your first day on the job as a career counselor and your boss asks you to prepare a memo that includes at least three suggested career options for the following three clients:

- A doctor who did well in medical school, but doesn't like to be near sick people
- A sports fanatic who will never be a professional athlete, but would like to work in the sports industry
- A theater buff, too self-conscious to act, but is extremely creative and has great artistic talents

Use resources such as this book (and other titles in the Career Ideas for Teens series) and O*NET Online (*http://online.onetcenter.org*) to find job titles that might fit with each client's skills and abilities.

includes an awareness of current "hot" careers and employment trends and the education requirements and skill sets associated with specific occupations, as well as understanding of the types of employers looking for specific types of employees. This doesn't mean that career counselors have to be walking encyclopedias of career information, but it does mean that they must know how to find the best career information available using resources such as the *Occupational Outlook Handbook* (*www.bls.gov/oco/home.htm*).

Whereas career counselors often start from scratch working with people (like students) who often have absolutely no clue about what they want to do, career coaches offer another, more specialized, type of career counseling. Their focus is on helping people who know what they want to do, but need help finding a path or specific job. Although some people use the terms interchangeably, career coaches are usually more focused on helping job hunters locate and obtain actual jobs (as opposed to careers) by helping with resume writing, interview techniques, and follow-up suggestions. Some career coaches work as matchmakers between local employers who need employees with certain qualifications and qualified clients who need jobs.

Career counselors may choose to specialize in any of several categories that serve clients of different ages or stages in their careers.

- In some high schools, the career counseling role may be filled by the guidance counselor or college advisor. In other schools, there may be a position with one of these titles: school to career coordinator, career education coordinator, career guidance specialist, career guidance technician, or career center technician.

High school career counselors show students options they may not be aware of that are in line with their interests and abilities. Counselors try to direct students to colleges or training programs where they can prepare for those options or to local companies that might be hiring in those areas.

- College career counselors work with the academic advisors. They ensure that the classes the students are being told to take are those that are most important to the employers who will eventually hire them. They may also arrange for corporate representatives to come to the campus to recruit students.
- Outplacement counselors are often hired by companies or industries that have to close a location or downsize, leading to a reduction of employees. Outplacement counselors also work with clients who have been successful in a field that may no longer need them and help them find ways to use their skills and experience to transition to a different career. Private career counselors serve the same function for individuals who do not have access to outplacement services through a former employer.
- Military career counselors are often tied in with recruiting and retention efforts, helping each individual find a career within the military that is right for him or her and eventually helping them transition to civilian life. Many military careers (commanding a nuclear submarine or managing the security of an embassy) require great skill and character, but do not have exact counterparts in the civilian world.
- Public career counseling centers may be funded by federal or state government programs, social service agencies, or community groups. Counselors in these centers may help people who have lost jobs, people making the transition from prison to outside life, or welfare recipients trying to get into the workforce.

find your **coach** future

coach Remember your first sports team? It may have been T-ball, soccer, basketball, or any of the other sports popular across America today. Chances are the coach of your first team was the mom or dad of one of your teammates. Maybe he or she once played that sport, or watches it on TV, or just wants to help out in the community.

Back then you learned that coaches are responsible for helping the players learn the skills, strategies, and rules of the game; working with individual players; keeping track of the equipment; scheduling practices; and teaching about sportsmanship and teamwork.

At the high school level, coaches are often teachers of physical education or other academic subjects in addition to coaching. They may have further responsibility for purchasing equipment, advising athletes on nutrition and training (both physical and mental), and even fund-raising for the team. Coaches may work with team sports, such as football or basketball, and individual sports, such as gymnastics or figure skating.

Coaching in a college environment is a much more specialized career. College coaches are usually trained and experienced professionals who may supervise a staff including scouts, specialized assistant coaches, and equipment managers. The higher the level in which the college competes, the more difficult the coach's job becomes, and the

Get Started Now!
- Volunteer to work with children's sports teams in your community.
- Play on as many community and school sports teams as you can without interfering with your schoolwork.
- Learn more about coaching specific sports at sites dedicated to those sports. For example: American Swimming Coaches Online at *www.swimmingcoach.org*, the Professional Skaters Association at *www.skatepsa.com*, or Fundamental Soccer at *www.fundamentalsoccer.com*.

Search It!
National High School Coaches Association at *www.nhsca.com* and National Collegiate Athletic Association (NCAA) at *www.ncaa.org*

Read It!
Find essential links to sports resources at *www.el.com/ elinks/sports*

Learn It!
- Bachelor's degree in physical education or sports management
- Experience playing sports in community, school, or professional programs

Earn It!
Median annual salary is $27,880. (Source: U.S. Department of Labor)

Find It!
Find information about available job opportunities at the National High School Coaches Association at *www.nhsca.com* and NCAA Online at *www.ncaa.org/ employment.html*.

higher the salary the coach can earn. For example, Indiana University hired Mike Davis in 2001 to coach its basketball team for four years, for total salary and incentives of more than $2 million! Bob Knight, the Indiana coach before Mike Davis, was hired by Texas Tech for six years with a total compensation package of $4.5 million.

Of course, neither of these coaches came into such top-level positions as a first job. Most coaches begin by playing the sport themselves, although they may not have been stars in their own playing days. They usually work their way up by coaching at high schools or at lower level colleges or as assistant coaches.

In addition to developing the individuals and the team to achieve a winning record, college coaches are responsible for:

- identifying and recruiting potential new players
- allocating money for travel, recruiting, and scholarships within predefined limits
- arranging meals, lodging, and buses or planes for games and recruiting
- knowing and implementing all NCAA rules and regulations
- helping the team during competitions by substituting players as needed, directing strategies, and calling plays

Even in the off-season, coaches are busy with recruiting, keeping athletes in good condition, and reviewing the prior season and planning for the next.

Hire Yourself!

Watch a college or professional game in the sport of your choice on TV. Keep the sound off. (Real coaches don't get to hear the commentators during the game, do they?) Pick a team and jot down notes about the team's strategies, strengths, and weaknesses. The next day, compare them to what sports writers and analysts say about the game in your local paper and in on-line news sources such as *Sports Illustrated* (**www.si.com**) and *USA Today* (**www.usatoday.com**). Use your findings to write a post-game briefing for the team that describes the high and low points of the game.

Being a good coach requires excellent people skills to motivate athletes to play their best and to recruit new players. Coaches must be able to communicate—to players, parents, and the school administration—and be organized to keep up with the administrative requirements. And, of course, they must be able to motivate their teams to win.

Coaching often requires a lot of travel. It also requires flexibility, as you may be changing jobs often. As Lou Holt said when he was the University of Arkansas football coach, "A lifetime contract for a coach means if you're ahead in the third quarter and moving the ball, they can't fire you."

college professor

Nearly 15 million full- and part-time students attend American colleges and universities today. That calls for a lot of full- and part-time college-level teachers! In fact, there are more than 1.3 million jobs in postsecondary education (including colleges, universities, and vocational-technical programs).

Teaching at the postsecondary level is quite different from teaching high school. For one thing, the classes are almost never the size of a high school class. College classes can be in large lecture halls with a few hundred students in the class. They can be small seminars, with five or 10 students who engage in spirited discussions with the teachers. Or, they can even be one-on-one, as a faculty member works with a student on a research project or independent study. Recently, many schools have begun to require their faculty to develop and manage on-line courses as well.

College and university faculty have many requirements to meet, in addition to the more obvious job components such as teaching undergraduate and graduate students, supervising teaching assistants, preparing lessons, and grading tests and papers. Most faculty members are considered experts in their fields. They need to be on top of the most recent developments in that field; consult with government, business, and other organizations when needed; conduct their own original research; and publish the results of their research. Many schools require

Search It!
American Association of University Professors: *www.aaup.org* and the Association of American Colleges and Universities *www.aacu-edu.org*

Read It!
Chronicle of Higher Education at *www.chronicle.com*. and at *www.aaup.org/Issues/index.htm*

Learn It!
- Doctoral degree (Ph.D.) is required for most tenured college and university professors
- Master's degree for associate professor opportunities
- Master's degree or bachelor's with experience for community college teachers

Earn It!
Salary varies by subject taught from $52,240 to $88,020. (Source: U.S. Department of Labor)

Find It!
The *Chronicle of Higher Education* lists many college positions at *www.chronicle.com/jobs*.

Get Started Now!
- Experiment with a wide variety of courses to find out which subject areas you find most interesting.
- Take advantage of every opportunity to hone your public speaking and writing skills in academic courses and after-school activities.
- Volunteer to provide peer tutoring services in one of your strongest subject areas.

Hire Yourself!

So what do college professors teach? Use the Internet (or resources available in your school's career guidance center) to look up the majors and academic subjects offered at two colleges or universities in your state. Make a list comparing the similarities and differences in the subject areas. Also try to find the number of faculty members at each institution and determine how many of those are full time, part time, and tenured.

their professors to publish a continuous and significant stream of original research in order to be granted tenure (lifetime employment). In academic communities, this is often referred to as the "publish or perish" requirement. Faculty members are also expected to serve on committees within the school and help determine school policies.

One challenge for many faculty members is allocating their time and resources between working with students and the research and publication that will help them gain highly-prized tenure. So, exactly how does tenure work? Faculty members are usually considered for tenure after working at a school for seven years. After a review of the teacher's record of teaching, research, and overall contribution to the institution, the school (and often its board of trustees) may vote to grant tenure.

Here's why tenure is so important to people teaching at the college level: A tenured professor cannot be fired without just cause and due process. The responsibility of a faculty member is to use the freedom of his or her office in an honest, courageous, and persistant effort to search out and communicate the truth that lies in the area of his or her competence. This brings us to a second benefit of the tenure system. The potential for job security makes the profession attractive to more people. Today, almost two-thirds of all full-time faculty members hold tenure, and most of the rest are working toward it.

Almost all tenured professors hold doctoral degrees, such as a Ph.D. A doctoral program usually takes an additional six to eight years schooling beyond a bachelor's degree. A doctoral program includes increasingly specialized courses and seminars, plus comprehensive examinations on all major areas of a particular field of study. In addition, candidates must complete a dissertation, which may take one to two years of full-time work. The dissertation is a book-length report detailing original research in the candidate's field of study and is supervised by one or more faculty advisors. In some fields, particularly the natural sciences, some students spend an additional two years on post-doctoral research and study before taking a faculty position.

According to the Bureau of Labor Statistics, the job outlook for post-secondary teachers should be much brighter than it has been in recent years. Employment is expected to grow much faster than the average for all occupations through 2012 due to the expected increase in the population of 18- to 24-year-olds. The best job prospects in colleges will continue to be in the computer sciences, engineering, and business fields. Growing opportunities are projected for a number of technical education programs as well as for professors who specialize in developing and managing distance learning programs.

find your future
cooperative extension agent

cooperative extension agent

How would you like to have an instant guide to doing anything and (almost) everything in your daily life? Do you know that your state provides just such a guide? The cooperative extension service of your state can tell you anything—from how to rewire a light switch to how to make homemade ice cream. The service can even tell you how to know when your Thanksgiving turkey is sufficiently cooked. It can provide month-by-month gardening guides for your part of the country, provide tips on calming a crying baby, teach you how to better manage your money, and give you advice on hunting for, cultivating, and cooking wild mushrooms.

Cooperative extension is the outreach and education arm of the Cooperative State Research, Education, and Extension Service (CSREES), part of the U.S. Department of Agriculture (USDA).

Cooperative extension evolved from the state university system, originally called the state land grant university system. These schools were created in each state to provide informal, off-campus public education, as well as more traditional on-campus programs. In the early

Search It!
National Association of County Agricultural Agents at *www.nacaa.com* and National Association of Agricultural Educators at *www.naae.org*

Read It!
Journal of Extension at *www.joe.org* and Living Well–Cooperative Extension at *www.learningandlivingwell.org/2nd/extension.htm*

Learn It!
Most jobs require at least a bachelor's degree in agriculture, consumer and family science, or education, as well as specific training and experience.

Earn It!
Median annual salary is $48,670. (Source: U.S. Department of Labor)

Find It!
See the Cooperative State Research, Education, and Extension Service (CSREES) - National Job Bulletin at *www.jobs.joe.org*.

Get Started Now!
- Get involved in your local 4-H program. Use your local phone book to look up the cooperative extension office serving your area and call for details.
- Use some of your elective credits to take courses in consumer studies, agriculture, or horticulture.
- Put your green thumb to the test by planting a garden, filling a windowsill container with herb plants, or nurturing a bed of flowers.

days of cooperative extension, the community education segment was directed primarily at rural communities, with an emphasis on agricultural education. Cooperative extension still provides many services to rural or agricultural communities, but its role has been expanded to include individuals, families, communities, and businesses in urban and suburban areas as well as rural ones. And, in addition to agricultural concerns, it addresses natural resources, neighborhood revitalization, water quality, health issues, public safety, youth development, school reform, concerns of local citizens, and economic growth.

Cooperative extension agents work within specified geographic areas, such as a county, to:

- provide information about improved methods of farming or ranching, including feeding and health maintenance of livestock; cultivation, growing, and harvesting practices; and budgeting
- teach about soil erosion or other environmental issues, wildlife management, or even marketing skills
- advise individuals and families on home management practices, such as budget planning, meal preparation, energy conservation, clothing care, and home furnishings
- develop and coordinate youth programs through the 4-H program

Extension agents may work with groups or individuals within their designated region, implementing programs, providing resources and information, and conducting lectures or workshops. They usually have offices someplace in the county, but they work wherever they are needed.

On the other hand, cooperative extension specialists are based at land grant college campuses or at state research stations and train the extension agents who work from the county offices. They plan and develop training materials, keep local agents up-to-date on new research, and coordinate activities at the state level. They also conduct research, prepare consumer information brochures, and may even produce films or radio and television programs.

Working as either an extension agent or an extension specialist requires the ability to work with different types of people (youth as well as adults) in different settings. It's important to be able to work as a team with colleagues and community members, to be able to build strong relationships in the community, and to be free to work evenings and weekends when necessary. As on-line education becomes more common, it is becoming more important to be comfortable with technology and computer skills.

find your future corporate trainer

corporate trainer

Just as teachers teach students, corporate trainers train employees. Generally working under the auspices of a company's human resources department, corporate trainers provide learning experiences designed to help employees work "smarter" and more productively.

There's nothing new about the fact that many companies have training sessions for their new employees. After all, even someone with experience at other companies needs to learn about the products, services, and procedures of a new workplace. The big change has been in the number of training sessions companies are providing for established employees.

Training can take place right in the workplace, at an outside facility, or even through on-line programs. The trainers may be in-house employees of the company, independent consultants with expertise in a specific area, or employees of another company that is providing equipment or technology to the company.

In general, training directors evaluate the organization's needs and develop training goals. They create a plan for accomplishing those goals and supervise all training efforts. Trainers may create their own teaching aids, or they may use books, films, or software created by materials development specialists. They may teach the classes themselves, or they

Get Started Now!
- Consider getting some early training experience by volunteering to teach a class at your place of worship or community center.
- Take on a part-time or summer job and pay attention to the methods and materials your new employer uses to train you.
- Visit the World Wide Learning website at *www.worldwidelearn.com* to investigate one of the fastest growing segments of corporate training: on-line learning.

Hire Yourself!

Loving Your Job magazine has just merged with *How to Succeed*. The two magazines had been engaged in fierce competition for the past 50 years, and the editors, writers, illustrators, and production workers are now unable to trust each other or work together. You have been brought in to oversee training for the new magazine. Experts in areas like technology and accounting will handle those specific areas. Your job is to unify the staff so that they are all loyal to the new company and able to combine their skills. Plan a six-hour day of team-building activities and exercises for the group. For ideas, go to **www.about.com** and search for team-building activities.

may hire classroom instructors for the actual sessions. Training can take place in short classes, in all-day (or multiple-day) seminars or workshops, or during industry conferences.

Almost every workplace is affected by the changes in technology. Things as simple as new copiers or a new phone system now require training for everyone at the workplace to take advantage of all the bells and whistles that are now part of the new equipment. Things that are more complex (such as computers and software) may require constant training.

Changes in the legal and business environments are other areas where training can be critical. A company can be at great risk if its employees do not know all of the implications of laws about sexual harassment, discrimination, accommodating the handicapped, safety precautions, accepting gifts from vendors, or discussing pricing with competitors. Because of the potential for expensive lawsuits and stiff fines, companies often bring in outside experts in these fields to do the training.

Corporate trainers are also used to help employees be more efficient, to smooth over some of the bumps that occur when companies merge and corporate cultures clash, and to help develop leadership skills so people can be promoted into management.

Whatever their area of specialization, effective trainers are good, clear communicators who are credible experts in the subjects that they teach. Becoming a corporate trainer usually requires at least as much work experience as it does formal training.

correctional educator

Search It!
Correctional Education Association at ***www.ceanational.org*** and National Institute for Correctional Education at ***www.iup.edu/NICE***

Read It!
From Incarceration to Productive Lifestyle at ***www.hudrivctr.org/iytrans.pdf***

Learn It!
For government-funded programs, most states require state teacher certification.

Earn It!
Median annual salary is $32,670. (Source: U.S. Department of Labor)

Find It!
Check with the Department of Corrections in your state and websites such as USAJOBS, the website of the U.S. Federal Government Office of Personal Management (***www.usajobs.opm.gov***), or the Bureau of Prisons (***www.bop.gov***).

correctional educator Teachers are no more immune to criminal activity (and prison sentences) than are doctors, lawyers, politicians, or other professionals. But some teachers actually choose to go to prison and don't even have to wear those orange jumpsuits while they're there!

Correctional institutions (jails, prisons, juvenile justice facilities, and community halfway houses) all have a stake in providing education for their residents. Many facilities see educating inmates not only as the right thing to do, but also as critical to maintaining smooth running of the facility and transition of inmates to outside life. Several studies have shown that prisoners who are released with greater literacy skills or actual job skills have a lower rate of recidivism (return to prison) and more success in becoming contributing members of society. In addition, other studies have shown that classes give inmates a chance to develop self-discipline,

Get Started Now!

- Volunteer to teach literacy at a community organization that works with low-income people.
- Learn about the correctional system in your state. Where are the institutions? What educational programs are currently offered?
- Find and read library books about others who have taught in prisons. Some suggestions: *Shakespeare Behind Bars: The Power of Drama in a Women's Prison*, by Jean Trounstine (New York: St Martin's Press, 2001); *Disguised As a Poem: My Years Teaching Poetry at San Quentin*, by Judith Tannenbaum (Boston: Northeastern University Press, 2000).

responsibility, a sense of competence and self-esteem, and a chance to relax and to have some contact with people from the "outside world."

Correctional educators may work with adults, juveniles, or people who qualify for special education services. Their students run the full gamut from total illiteracy to those who want to earn college or graduate degrees and, depending on the class and where it's taught, may include students who signed up voluntarily, students who were required to take that class, and students who needed to have good behavior to earn the right to participate. Correctional officers work with offenders who can come from the full gamut of correctional life—from minimum security to death row.

Youthful offenders are subject to the same educational privileges and requirements as they would have been had they remained in the public schools. Often, their educational needs are met by their local school district. In some cases, the prisons in an area might actually be designated as a school district of their own.

The other major types of correctional education include:

- General literacy education: Many correctional institutions mandate basic literacy for inmates who are below eigth-grade levels in reading, math, or language skills.
- GED (general equivalency diploma or general education development) programs: Some correctional systems require achievement of GED credentials in order to qualify for parole; other systems provide GED and English as a second language classes for those who choose to take them.
- Vocational or technical education: Correctional institutions may work with local community colleges to give instruction in various skills and trades (including areas as diverse as barbering, carpentry, ceramics, culinary arts, and welding).

- Life skills education: Programs that seek to help the inmate return to society may include job-seeking skills, parenting, anger management, bill paying, and so on.
- Creative education: Many institutions offer classes in art, music, dance, or theater.

What does it take to be a correctional educator? For one thing, you will be working with a population unlike most that you have probably known. You must be patient and open to working with many different cultures and ethnic groups. Most states require state teaching certification for government-sponsored literacy and GED classes. Some require substantial prior experience (a minimum of 10 years in Massachusetts). Federal prisons permit different combinations of education and experience to qualify to teach there. Teachers of life skills or cultural programs may be volunteers (as in the Girl Scouts Behind Bars program), or may work with a local college, or may be funded by a nonprofit organization (such as the arts programs sponsored by the Philadelphia Museum of Art or Florida's Art Behind Bars).

education attorney

By the time most kids reach second or third grade, they know enough about our legal system to shout with conviction, "It's a free country, and I can do whatever I want."

We do live in a free country, but that freedom comes with limitations and responsibilities. Our country values education so highly that legal questions regarding public school education have been taken all the way up to the Supreme Court, and Congress has enacted many pieces of legislation that affect how our schools function.

It's likely that your own school or town has already faced questions of school-related rights and responsibilities. Do any of these questions sound familiar to you?

- Can a student be suspended because the school considers the picture or writing on his T-shirt offensive?
- Can schools ban books they don't like?
- Must students submit to random drug testing?
- How far can schools go with zero-tolerance rules?

Get Started Now!

- Get involved in peer mediation at your school.
- Sign up for debate and speech classes and consider joining your school's debate team.
- Talk to the special needs coordinator at your school to find out more about the types of accommodations available to students with special needs.
- Check the website of your state bar association to see if they have an education law committee. If they do, write or call to ask for materials about educational law.

Search It!
American Bar Association at **www. abanet.org** and Wrightslaw at Special Education Law & Advocacy at **www.wrightslaw.com**

Read It!
Education Law–MegaLaw.com at **www.megalaw.com/top/ education.php** and the Center for Law and Education at **www. cleweb.org**

Learn It!
- Bachelor's degree in any area with heavy emphasis on writing, public speaking, reading, researching, and logic
- Three-year law school degree
- Successful completion of state bar exam

Earn It!
Median annual salary is $105,890. (Source: U.S. Department of Labor)

Find It!
Most educational lawyers have their own firm, work for a separate department of a larger law firm, or work for a city or school board.

Hire Yourself!

A group of high school students has hired you to help them prove that many of the rules in their school violate the Bill of Rights. Their main concerns are freedom of the press (they want their school newspaper to be free of review or censorship by the school), freedom of expression (the school should not regulate what they wear), and freedom from unreasonable search and seizure (the school should not be able to check backpacks, purses, or lockers).

Write an argument supporting each of the students' ideas. Then see how your arguments compare to the ones used in actual cases. Check out How Do Students' Rights Compare to Adults' Rights?, New Jersey v. T.L.O., Landmark Supreme Court Cases, at *www.landmarkcases.org/newjersey/compare.html*.

- Do parents have the right to home-school their children? What safeguards ensure that the child is getting an adequate education?
- Can school boards force schools to teach some subjects (like sex education) or prohibit them from teaching others (like evolution)?
- Can schools insist that students wear uniforms?

Some lawyers (also known as attorneys) represent students, parents, or teachers in these types of cases; others represent the schools or school districts. Both are generally experts on constitutional law, have studied education law in depth, and are familiar with all the similar cases that have already been decided.

Our country has laws guaranteeing a "fair and appropriate public education" to all children, regardless of handicaps, special needs, race, income, or religious beliefs. Some educational lawyers choose to work with parents who feel that the schools may not be providing appropriate programs for their children who have physical, emotional, behavioral, or learning disabilities. These lawyers usually work with a team that includes educational advocates—people who are not attorneys, but who are well acquainted with the systems and procedures of the school system.

Together, the educational lawyer and the advocate help parents negotiate with schools to implement the accommodations called for in IDEA (Individuals with Disabilities Education Act) and in Section 504 of the Vocational Rehabilitation Act, and they teach parents how to be more active and effective advocates for themselves. They may help arrange

testing and evaluation of the child, interpret the results for the parent, set up IEPs (Individualized Educational Programs), attend meetings at the school, and represent the child's interests in court if necessary.

Education law has become so important that many law schools now provide specialized programs in that area, and some offer law students opportunities to volunteer in the field.

However, competition for the best jobs will continue to be keen throughout the coming years. Good training, the best grades, and focused goals can combine to open doors for prospective education lawyers.

elementary school teacher

elementary school teacher

Elementary school teachers play such a huge role in children's lives that it's likely that your parents and grandparents even now can remember the names of their elementary school teachers more easily than their high school or college teachers!

During the school day, the elementary school teacher's main job is to give students a firm foundation in the basics of reading, math, science, social studies, and language arts. Today, most classrooms are interactive, with discussions, group work, and hands-on learning experiences. Good teachers are creative in planning learning activities that engage students. They are able to communicate clearly and engagingly, help students learn specific content, and teach students how to work together, think logically, and solve problems.

While at school, the elementary school teacher is also responsible for identifying and referring students with physical, emotional, or learning

Get Started Now!

● Start working with young children now. Be a tutor. Work in a day camp or after school program. Help in a community center.
● Enroll in child development and developmental psychology classes.
● See if your school has a chapter of Future Educators of America. These clubs are organized by Phi Delta Kappa International, the professional educators association, to help students explore careers in education. Check out Phi Delta Kappa Student Activities at *www.pdkintl.org/studser/fea.htm*.

Hire Yourself!

The board of education in your town has just hired you to be a new first grade teacher. Fortunately you have the whole summer to prepare. Start off by planning your first day of school. How are you going to set up the room? What resources will you have in the room, how will desks and chairs be arranged, what will you use to decorate the room? How will you help the students get to know each other and feel comfortable in their new class? What kinds of discipline and other structure will you set up? Write a letter to the parents of your students, introducing yourself and telling them about your plans for the first day of school.

disabilities; meeting with parents, supervisors, and other teachers; decorating classrooms and hallway bulletin boards; supervising lunch and playground time; planning and escorting class trips; celebrating birthdays and holidays; encouraging curiosity, love of learning, and a desire to try your best; preparing students for standardized tests and administering those tests; supporting students through everything from the birth of a sibling to a parents' divorce to losing a baby tooth in class.

Elementary school teachers may also coach a team, direct a school play or choir, prepare an art exhibit, or provide after-school homework help.

After school, teachers are still very busy. They need to plan lessons; design and correct tests and homework; complete report cards and write comments; find new ways to create exciting, stimulating projects and activities; read professional materials about teaching techniques, classroom management, and their area of specialization; and take continuing education classes.

There are several different types of elementary schools.

- Private schools, which must be accredited by an approved state or regional association, are independent of the state or local district.
- District schools (most public schools) are those whose students have been assigned there based on their address.
- Charter schools, another type of public school, are run by groups of teachers, parents, and/or foundations, rather than by the local school board. Charter schools are often tailored to specific community needs and may be free of many district regulations.
- Magnet schools are also publicly funded and are a part of the regular school district. Each magnet school focuses on a particular

discipline, such as science, mathematics, arts, or computer science. Magnet schools were originally created to use their special focus to attract students from other parts of the school district, thereby aiding voluntary school desegregation.

To succeed in an elementary school teaching career, a person must have the right personality. Young children expect their teachers to be warm, patient, caring, even-tempered, and enthusiastic every day of the year. Physical fitness is important for elementary school educators as well—it takes a lot of energy and stamina to keep up with a room full of young students! Teaching may not be as easy as it sometimes looks from the outside, but it is a challenging and rewarding career. Most teachers would not do anything else!

The U.S. Department of Labor says that job opportunities for teachers over the next 10 years should be excellent, attributable mostly to the large number of teachers expected to retire.

find english as a second language (ESL) instructor your future

Search It!
Teachers of English to Speakers of Other Languages (TESOL) at *www.tesol.org* and National Center for ESL Literacy Education (NCLE) at *www.cal.org/ncle*

Read It!
Frequently asked question (FAQ) section of NCLE website at *www.cal.org/ncle/FAQS.HTM* and Internet TESL Journal at *http://iteslj.org*

Learn It!
● Bachelor's or master's degree in education, linguistics, or related major
● Some states require special ESL certification

Earn It!
The average salary is $41,470. (Source: U.S. Department of Labor)

Find It!
Find postings for ESL teaching positions at the *Chronicle of Higher Education* website at *www. chronicle.com* and Internet TESL Journal at *http://iteslj.org*.

english as a second language (ESL) instructor

English is a really easy language to speak, read, and understand—IF you grew up with it. For people from other countries and cultures, English can be incredibly difficult. For one thing, English often does not follow standardized rules. Take a nice, easy verb, like "to see." We say, "I see, he sees, you see." No problem. Then look at a verb like "to be." That becomes, "I am, he is, you are." No rhyme or reason to it at all! And then there are English nouns. You can have one house or two houses. BUT…one mouse or two mice. Where's the logic?

There are several different terms for people who teach English to non-native speakers. Jobs in this field may be listed under ESL (English as a second language) teachers, ESOL (English for speakers of other languages) teachers, or EFL (English as a foreign language) teachers.

Get Started Now!
● Ask if you can sit in on (or even help out in) a class where ESL is taught to adults. Look at community organizations (like the YMCA) and adult education programs offered at community centers or in a community college.
● Study a foreign language as part of your academic program to gain an understanding of what it takes to speak and read in another language.
● Watch the news or a soap opera in another language. Keep a journal of how it feels to guess meanings from actions and facial expressions.

Hire Yourself!

Imagine that you've just been certified as an ESL teacher. You're young and adventurous and decide you'd like to work in another country for your first ESL teaching assignment. Go on-line to ***www.eflweb.com*** and click on Travel Zone. Make a chart comparing the various characteristics of at least three different countries. Use a highlighter to indicate where you'd most like to work.

Often, countries where English is not usually spoken (like China or Russia) consider it a foreign language, and primarily English-speaking countries (like the United States or Australia) consider it a second language for non-native speakers.

Whatever you call it, teaching the English language is something you have to be trained to do—the mere fact that you speak English well does not qualify you to teach it to others.

Teachers of English to non-native speaking students have a world of opportunities open to them. They can teach in countries around the world, in elementary or secondary schools, in colleges and universities, or in adult education programs. They can teach children, businessmen, or immigrants to a new country. Some ESL teachers in the United States work with children in a regular school classroom. Others teach adults in a community college or community-based program. ESL teachers may also teach classes specialized toward a specific purpose, such as helping foreign-born doctors converse with patients about symptoms or teaching engineering students the English vocabulary for that profession.

Teaching English in other countries may mean working with children and adolescents in school settings, much like your own French or Spanish teacher does here. Or it may involve working in a university or for a company that sends its executives abroad or for a commercial language school. Salaries for teaching in other countries may be low, and teachers often have to provide their own transportation to that country. On the other hand, it is an excellent opportunity to really get to know another country and culture, and living expenses are often far lower than in the United States.

Many countries prefer that British English rather than American English be taught. In those cases, instructors who grew up speaking American English have to learn British spelling and vocabulary themselves before they can teach their students.

find your environmental educator future

environmental educator

Work outdoors! Save the earth! Teach children, adults, and companies to care about our environment! As an environmental educator, you can do all these things—and more.

Environmental education is a huge and varied field. It is an active profession that, on any given day, may involve hiking, diving, climbing, or canoeing with students. And environmental educators do most of their work during weekends and vacations, when people are available to see them. It's a career for nature lovers and involves working with plants, animals, and insects of the environment you are teaching about. Here are just some of the careers that are available:

- Educators who work in environmental centers create, coordinate, and teach programs for teachers, as well as for students. They may work indoors in labs or classrooms at their centers or outdoors near local streams, watersheds, or other areas. Environmental educators in these positions need a minimum of a bachelor's degree in environmental science, usually combined with a degree in education.
- Park rangers work in our national parks. Some park rangers specialize in fee collection or law enforcement, but other park rangers

Get Started Now!
- Look into summer job opportunities in a park or nature center.
- Take classes in CPR and first aid.
- Take up an outdoor activity like hiking, canoeing, and other outdoor sports.

Search It!
North American Association for Environmental Education at *www.naaee.org*

Read It!
Natural Wonders: A Guide to Early Childhood for Environmental Educators at *www.seek.state. mn.us/classrm_e.cfm* and find a variety of resources through EE Link at *www.eelink.net/ professionalresources.html*

Learn It!
Most jobs require a minimum of a bachelor's degree.

Earn It!
Median annual salary is $37,370. (Source: U.S. Department of Labor)

Find It!
Find out about employment opportunities at Environmental Jobs and Careers at *www.ecoemploy.com* and the Environmental Careers Organization website at *www. eco.org*.

Hire Yourself!

Yitou have been hired as an environmental educator for your county. Your assignment is to focus on a specific environmental issue that is important to your part of the world. For background information go on-line to the Sierra Club website at *www.sierraclub.com* and click on the "my backyard" icon for timely information about local issues. Prepare a presentation for either young children or teens that includes:
- an explanation of the problem
- suggested solutions

Make sure to incorporate hands-on activities and attractive visuals to make your presentation interesting and memorable.

are environmental educators called naturalists or interpreters. They give talks in visitor centers, set up exhibits, or provide guided hikes and campfire programs. They also help protect plants and animals in the parks, wildlife refuges, and nature preserves. At least a two-year associate's degree is required for these types of positions. Training in CPR and advanced first aid or emergency medical technician (EMT) certification is very helpful.

- Marine biologists with training in education may work with state and national programs to coordinate marine and coastal educational efforts. They organize beach and underwater cleanups, monitor species like sea turtles, lead manatee dive trips, run estuary canoe trips, and teach groups about recycling and other ways to help the marine environment. Marine environment educators should have a graduate degree in science education or environmental education, as well as an undergraduate degree in a relevant science field.

- Corporate environmental educators work with companies and industries to promote responsible attitudes toward the environment. They may visit large and small companies to show them how their products or manufacturing processes affect the environment and help them make changes that are environmentally positive. Corporate educators must have a minimum of a bachelor's degree, as well as excellent analytical and presentation skills.

- Consumer educators create brochures, radio and television programs, and newspaper and magazine articles to help people understand the impact of their choices on the environment.

Consumer educators often bring issues to the attention of the public that may influence the kinds of purchases people make. Smokey Bear is an example of one of the most well-known environmental awareness programs. For more than 50 years, Smokey has been educating the public about forest fire safety, and the National Association of State Foresters (***www.stateforesters.org***) continues to create new materials for Smokey. Consumer environmental educators need at least a bachelor's degree and often a graduate degree in education.

There is a lot of competition for most environmental education jobs. Good training, a history of volunteering, and experience in related fields such as teaching often pave the way for landing a job to help protect the environment through education and awareness.

fitness trainer

Search It!
American College of Sports Medicine (ACSM) at **www.acsm.org** and American Council on Exercise at **www.acefitness.org**

Read It!
Find articles from the National Strength and Conditioning Association (NSCA) at **http://nsca.allenpress.com/nscaonline/?request=index-html**

Learn It!
- Bachelor's or master's degree in a field like exercise science or physical education
- Certification in areas of specialization such as aerobics, fitness, yoga, or kickboxing

Earn It!
Median annual salary is $49,510. (Source: U.S. Department of Labor)

Find It!
Jobs are listed at the websites of the American Council on Exercise (**www.acefitness.org**) and the National Strength and Conditioning Association (**www.nsca.com**).

fitness trainer Fitness training is one of those rare career opportunities where a person gets paid to work out, eat right, and keep fit. Fitness training is a relatively new concept. Even your grandparents or great-grandparents might not have understood the concept of formal exercise.

These days, commuting, desk jobs, and leisure time activities like TV, movies, and surfing the net seem to conspire to help people "spread out" rather than "bulk up." Increasing awareness of the pitfalls of a sedentary lifestyle is drawing increasing numbers of people into gyms and fitness centers, thus creating a growing need for fitness professionals.

Fitness training means different things to different people. There are different job titles and different levels of training and professionalism. In general, fitness trainers help their clients assess their level of physical fitness and help them set and reach fitness goals. Trainers demon-

Get Started Now!
- Get a head start on some of the courses you'll have to take as you prepare for a career as a fitness trainer. Learn as much as you can about basic anatomy, first aid, and nutrition.
- Check out various gyms or health clubs in your town to compare the differences in their approach to fitness training. Most facilities display the college and graduate degrees of their trainers, as well as their certifications. Tour some facilities and compare the backgrounds of their trainers.
- Consider accepting any job at a fitness center. Even if you're answering the phone or washing the towels, you'll make good contacts and be able to learn more about how trainers work with different types of clients.
- Take a variety of physical education courses at your school.

strate various exercise activities and model proper techniques. A big part of the job is motivating clients to safely push their limits until they've achieved their personal best.

Fitness training can go far beyond staying in shape and preventing future disease. It can be a critical part of a recovery or rehabilitation program for people who have chronic illnesses or are recovering from treatments for illnesses. The highest level of certification (the ACSM Registered Clinical Exercise Physiologist) allows trainers to work with clients who are referred by and are under the continued care of a licensed physician. These clients may be elderly people, children, or pregnant women or they may have heart, lung, immunity, nerve, or muscle problems. The fitness programs for these clients are designed to have therapeutic or functional benefits and to educate them for the future. Achieving this level of certification requires a graduate degree in exercise science, physiology, or exercise physiology and at least 1,200 hours of relevant clinical experience (with specific requirements in cardiovascular, pulmonary, metabolic, orthopedic/musculoskeletal, neuromuscular, and immunological/hematological situations).

A more traditional situation for fitness training is a commercial or hospital fitness studio,

where clients pay a monthly fee to work out on their own or take classes such as aerobics or spinning. Fitness trainers who want to run a business without a ton of administrative headaches might look for a personal training studio, where individual trainers can rent space and maintain their independent businesses. Those looking for a direct connection to the health field might explore opportunities with a clinically oriented facility, where clients are required to work out with their own physical therapist or a certified trainer from the facility. Clinically oriented fitness centers help clients who are more at-risk (those coming out of chemotherapy or with diseases like Parkinson's) safely return to an active and fit lifestyle and often integrate nutritional education to address the client's total health outlook. Trainers need more advanced education and experience to work at a clinically oriented center.

Fitness trainers not only help people look better and feel better, they also help them prevent and recover from illness. With widespread concern about growing rates of obesity among both children and adults in this country and increasing emphasis on the health benefits associated with fitness, there's plenty of opportunity on the horizon for fitness trainers.

guidance counselor

If you're in high school now, you may think of your school guidance counselor as the person to go to for changes in your class schedule or to get a college application. In fact, those activities are only a small part of the high school guidance counselor's job.

At all grade levels, school counselors work to create an atmosphere of safety and trust in dealing with the students. Counselors may meet with classes as a whole, with individual students, or with small groups of students. They help students understand and manage social, behavioral, and personal issues.

In elementary schools, guidance counselors observe individual children, trying to identify issues that can be helped through early identification and intervention. Children in elementary school are not only facing the academic challenges of school, but are also learning a lot about themselves and developing attitudes and ways of interacting with peers, family, and the school itself. When guidance counselors become aware of current or potential problems, they work with the parent and school team to develop strategies that will help both in the classroom and in the home. Some of the issues school counselors may address with children include: use of illegal substances, coping strategies, communication, family issues, peer group issues, social skills, and conflict resolution.

Get Started Now!

- Arrange to interview a guidance counselor in your school. Try to make a list of all of the things he or she does in a typical day.
- Include psychology and communication courses in your school schedule.
- Get involved in peer mediation or peer tutoring programs available through your school or community center.

Search It!
American School Counselor Association at *www.schoolcounselor.org*, American Counseling Association at *www.counseling.org*, and American College Counseling Association at *www.collegecounseling.org*

Read It!
Counseling Today at your library or on-line in the "publications" section of *www.counseling.org* and *Journal of Counseling & Development* (JCD) at *www.counseling.org/site/PageServer?pagename=publications_jcd_jcd*

Learn It!
- Master's degree and in some cases classroom teaching experience
- State certification (varies by state)

Earn It!
Median annual salary is $46,160. (Source: U.S. Department of Labor)

Find It!
Look at local and state school district advertising and websites.

Hire Yourself!

As a high school guidance counselor, one of your main jobs is to help students set realistic goals for their future. Find materials that would help you in the following situation: Jim loves some of the shows on TV like *CSI* and wants to be a forensic scientist. He is very creative in problem solving, but has shown no ability in physics or chemistry, and he gets creeped out by dead bodies. How will you help him understand what forensic science is really about? What can you do to help him find career ideas that appeal to his interests and are a better match for his proven abilities?

You can use the Internet or library resources to find information about the qualifications of forensic scientists as well as information about career guidance strategies. Keep your ideas positive and encouraging.

Write a note to Jim's family, explaining what advice you gave to their child.

The elementary school guidance counselor may refer students or families to the school social worker, school psychologist, or to outside agencies.

Middle school students are especially affected by the physical, social, and psychological transitions that happen during those years. School guidance counselors again provide a safe and trusting atmosphere for students to seek help and support during these times. Middle school guidance counselors also help students think about their long-term goals, especially where there is a choice of high schools for them to apply to. And, as in elementary schools, the guidance counselor leads the team of parents, teachers, and other school specialists to develop appropriate programs for students with special needs.

High school guidance counselors address an extremely diverse set of challenges. In some schools, separate counselors or technicians are provided for help with career exploration and college applications. In other schools, the guidance counselor must do it all. Some school districts see guidance counselors as fulfilling more of a "mental-health" role. Those districts look to guidance counselors to identify students who may commit violence in school, work with other disciplinary cases, help students with substance abuse problems, coordinate programs for pregnant teens, or reduce the number of school dropouts. Other districts look to counselors as the people who will help guide each student to his or her best future. In that scenario, guidance counselors focus on helping students decide on their post-high school plans, ensuring that they complete the requirements for the jobs they want or the colleges or training programs they want to attend. In either model, guidance counselors are often called upon to make and adjust class schedules; disseminate information about careers, colleges, and admissions tests; coordinate college and/or career fairs; have applications for financial aid; and more.

find your future

instructional coordinator

If you have friends in other parts of your state, you may have noticed that they often study the same topics as you do in each subject area. Coincidence? Not really. It's all due to the work of the instructional coordinators or, as they are sometimes called, curriculum specialists.

Curriculum usually refers to the material taught in a subject, and school districts often have a specialist for each area. The term curriculum is also used to describe the sequence of courses students have to take, and instructional coordinators have a hand in developing that too. Some instructional coordinators specialize in specific subject areas. Others specialize in different groups of students, focusing on students at the elementary, middle, or high school levels or working with programs for special education or gifted students.

As hard as they try, teachers just can't keep up with everything that happens in the subject areas they teach. New guidelines come down from state and local governments, telling schools what students need to know in order to graduate or to pass standardized tests. Researchers find

Get Started Now!

- Pay attention to the various textbooks and materials you use in each of your classes. Notice the different approaches they use to help students learn.
- Ask a favorite teacher to explain the curriculum guidelines and lesson plans they use to keep your class on track.
- Consider working at a child care center or summer day camp for children to get an understanding of how teachers plan learning activities.

Hire Yourself!

You have been hired as instructional coordinator of a small private elementary school. The director of the school has asked you to develop a five-lesson curriculum unit to teach first grade students about the solar system. Visit websites such as the PBS Teacher Source at *www.pbs. org/teachersource* and the Mid-continent Research for Education and Learning at *www.mcrel.org* to find ideas. Print out instructions and visuals, and compile them in your own curriculum guide.

more effective ways to help students understand certain concepts. Changes in national policy or the outlook in the job market create needs to emphasize different things. And changes in technology sometimes leave older teachers wondering how they will catch up to their own students. Fortunately, instructional coordinators help fill in those gaps.

Instructional coordinators review the educational programs in each school or department to make sure that what is being taught meets the required goals and standards. They also evaluate the teaching methods and techniques used in the classroom to make sure students' needs are being met. In addition, they conduct training with teachers to share the best teaching practices and to learn about new teaching techniques.

Much of an instructional coordinator's work does not involve working directly with students or teachers at all. When schools buy textbooks, lab equipment, or other instructional materials, they invest huge amounts of money in something that will be with the school for many years to come. The instructional coordinator reviews all of the available options, confers with teachers, and recommends the products that will be most valuable in meeting the school's goals and the students' needs.

Curriculum is always evolving and changing. The instructional coordinator watches for these changes, helps the teachers get up to speed, and makes sure the instructional materials in the school are still appropriate. Changes in curriculum often result from changes in social attitudes. Today, even pre-K classrooms use books that reflect the diversity of our society, acknowledging the contributions of people from all ethnic and cultural groups. Even the literature we study reflects the different types of experiences that real people have.

Changes in technology also require changes in curriculum. As computers, and later the Internet, became common in work and home situations, teachers had to learn how to use them and how to teach students to use them. And finally, new problems in the world mean new needs in school curriculum. HIV/AIDS awareness, for example, is now critical for teachers to understand and teach.

The instructional coordinator, whose job is to keep up with all the news in education, is the person who can train teachers in school, find courses for them to attend, and locate appropriate materials to help them teach most effectively.

Not all instructional coordinators work in schools. Some work at the district or state level and help develop the standards that the local coordinators will help implement. Others work in the business world. There, they help develop textbooks, educational videos, teacher guides, and other supplemental materials, making sure that all content is factually correct, that all activities are educationally sound, and that the material meets state goals and standards.

find your librarian future

librarian

Librarians are dull, boring people, who put books back on shelves and tell people to be quiet, right? Wrong! In fact, librarians can be some of the most interesting people you will ever meet! Librarians have a wide choice of places to work. Although most of the 120,000 libraries in the United States are in schools (see the profile for School Media Specialist), there are thousands of public libraries, academic (college and university) libraries, and libraries for the U.S. government, the armed forces, corporations, prisons, and other specialized purposes.

Different types of librarian jobs require different emphasis on the three main aspects of the job: user services, technical services, and administrative services.

Reference and children's librarians devote most of their time to user services, helping people find the information they need and teaching them how to access information. To do their job well, librarians must have very good interview skills. Imagine a student who wants help finding information about Benjamin Franklin. A good librarian will be able to find out what he really needs. The information might be for a project on the lives of famous people or how people lived in colonial America; it could be about Franklin's contributions to the Declaration of Independence, what he accomplished as an ambassador to France, his inventions, or how modern life is based on his early ideas. By helping

Search It!
American Library Association (ALA) at **www.ala.org**, Special Libraries Association (SLA) at **www.sla.org**, and Public Library Association (PLA) at **www.pla.org**

Read It!
American Library and other periodicals at **www.ala.org** and *Library Journal* at **www.libraryjournal.com**

Learn It!
Master's of library science (MLS)

Earn It!
Median annual salary is $44,430. (Source: U.S. Department of Labor)

Find It!
Find library job postings at **www.libraryjobpostings.org**.

Get Started Now!

- Check out your local library—and not just the books. Consider attending some of the community events they sponsor or joining (or starting) a teen book club.
- Find out about opportunities to job shadow, intern, or volunteer at your local library.
- Read! Expand your literary horizons and try new kinds of books—both fiction and nonfiction.

Hire Yourself!

Congratulations! Your town's library has just hired you as the youth advisor for the teen summer reading program. Your job is to create a list of 10 books of interest to this age group. The challenge is in choosing books with wide appeal to both male and female readers with an interesting mix of genres. Use resources like your local library (of course), the Young Adult Library Services section of the American Library Association website at *www.ala.org*, and the on-line bookstore Amazon at *www.amazon.com*.

Make a flyer announcing your choices that libraries can distribute to its young adult patrons.

the student define the question, a good librarian can save a lot of time and dead-end searches.

Other librarians focus on the technical services side, which involves acquiring materials, cataloging resources, and preparing them for use. Most librarians have a limited budget, so librarians have to be able to prioritize the purchases that will do the most good for the library and its users.

A third area that some librarians focus on is administrative services. Administrative librarians are like the executive managers of the library. They oversee the management and planning of libraries; negotiate contracts for services, materials, and equipment; supervise library employees; perform public relations and fund-raising duties; prepare budgets; and direct activities to ensure that everything functions properly.

Public libraries often make a big difference in the communities in which they are located. They may run bookmobiles to areas that don't have nearby branches, have "movie nights," run workshops on finding jobs or other topics, encourage reading, promote adult literacy classes, and host authors or other guest speakers to stimulate interest in reading.

While public libraries serving the general needs of a local population are among the most commonly known type of library, there are also a variety of highly specialized libraries. Law, medical, and music libraries are all examples of specialized libraries.

All libraries, no matter their focus, are going through an especially exciting era of change. The traditional concept of a library is being redefined from a place to access paper records or books, to one which also houses the most advanced media, including CD-ROM, the Internet, virtual libraries, and remote access to a wide range of resources. Consequently, librarians increasingly are combining traditional duties with tasks involving quickly changing technology.

find your future library technician

library technician

Want to work in a library without waiting to complete a master's degree? Becoming a library technician is the perfect way to get into the field, experience an enjoyable job (if you're a real research-lover or book-lover), and have a way to check out library careers before committing to two years of graduate school.

Most library technicians work in school, academic, or public libraries. Some work in hospital, corporate, or medical libraries; others work for the federal government (especially the Department of Defense and the Library of Congress) or state and local governments. Library technicians also staff bookmobiles—trucks loaded with books that visit designated sites on a regular schedule. Bookmobiles bring the library to people who may find it inconvenient or impossible to get to the regular library location.

The library technician's main job is to help libraries function smoothly. They help librarians acquire new materials and then process those materials when they arrive—entering catalog information into the library's computer, coding library materials, preparing books for binding, organizing and maintaining periodical collections, and updating databases and Web pages. They also provide orientations for new users, remove out-dated and unused materials from the collections, and help visitors find the books or information they need. Library technicians may

Get Started Now!

- Visit a variety of libraries in your area—public, school, and others you may discover through a little research.
- Volunteer to work in your school library or a public library.
- Take computer courses at school to build your technical skills.

Search It!
American Library Association (ALA) at *www.ala.org*, and Council on Library/Media Technicians (COLT) at *http://colt.ucr.edu*

Read It!
Associates: The Electronic Library Support Staff Journal at *www.associates.ucr.edu*, *American Library* and other periodicals listed on the ALA website at *www.ala.org*, and *Library Journal* in print or at *www.libraryjournal.com*

Learn It!
- High school diploma or general equivalency diploma (GED)
- Some employers require an associate's or bachelor's degree, and many require work experience

Earn It!
Median annual salary is $25,280. (Source: U.S. Department of Labor)

Find It!
Library job postings at *www. libraryjobpostings.org* or at your local library.

Hire Yourself!

Visit your school or local public library and figure out the best process for finding resources—whether it's via computer or a card catalog. Make a poster describing the process in a clear and simple way. Be sure to follow your own directions to see if they work!

teach visitors how to use microfilm readers or how to access the Internet, design posters and other displays, or run children's programs.

Library technicians who work in specialized government libraries or in corporations, museums, or research centers may also conduct literature searches, compile bibliographies, and prepare abstracts (summaries of articles).

Library assistants (another job option for library work) perform more clerical tasks, such as sorting returned books and other materials and puting them back on the shelves. They locate materials for individuals or for loans to other libraries. Library assistants help visitors find books, issue them library cards, and help them check out or return materials. They help care for library materials by taping torn book pages, repairing covers, or using other specialized methods for videos, CDs, and more valuable materials.

Some library assistants help visitors with vision problems. The library assistant reviews the list of materials the visitors wants, then finds versions, or closely related substitutes, that are in Braille, large type, or on casette tapes.

Technology is expected to spur job growth among library technicians. This is true because computers have simplified certain tasks, such as descriptive cataloging, which can now be handled by technicians instead of librarians. For example, technicians can now easily retrieve information from a central database and store it in the library's computer. The U.S. Department of Labor also expects increased use of special libraries by professionals and other workers, which would in turn result in the growth of job opportunities for library technicians in those settings.

museum educator

Quick! Name three kinds of museums. What did you come up with? You probably included an art museum, maybe one devoted to natural history, and possibly an interactive science museum. Another common type of museum is the historical museum, which may have exhibits about how a city, state, or region developed; or may tell the story of a single person, such as a president or other figure; or may focus on a very specific place and its role in history or in the life of a person (such as Pearl Harbor and World War II or Thomas Jefferson and his home, Monticello). Some special museums have exhibits about the history of a product, such as the automobile (the Henry Ford Museum in Dearborn, Michigan) or a pastime (like the Baseball Hall of Fame in Cooperstown, New York).

A museum can be on an aircraft carrier (like the Intrepid Sea-Air-Space Museum in New York), a re-creation of an actual village (like Williamsburg, Virginia, or Plymouth Plantation, Massachusetts), or a working factory (like the Corning Museum of Glass in Corning, New York). Zoos, aquariums, and nature centers are also considered to be museums.

According to the American Association of Museums, museums spend about $4.1 billion a year on educational programming, exhibits, and research, and an additional $1.1 billion to care for the objects and living specimens in their collections. In total, there are about 865 million

Get Started Now!

- Visit as many museums as possible to get a better sense of how they present information to various audiences including children and adults.
- Use some of your elective courses to explore your interest areas, whether your interests focus on art, music, science, or whatever.

Search It!
Smithsonian Institute: Training Programs in Museum Studies at *http://museumstudies.si.edu/ TrainDirect.htm*

Read It!
Smithsonian Center for Education and Museum Studies at *http:// museumstudies.si.edu* and Museum Stuff at *www. museumstuff.com*

Learn It!
- Bachelor's degree in education or in a subject related to a museum, such as art or science
- Graduate degree in museum studies

Earn It!
Median annual salary is $35,270. (Source: U.S. Department of Labor)

Find It!
Find leads on museum jobs at *www.museumjobs.com*, National Trust for Historic Preservation at *www.nationaltrust. org*, and Museum Employment Resource Center at *www. museum-employment.com*.

Hire Yourself!

Look at the current exhibits featured on-line at the web-sites of the Metropolitan Museum of Art (*www.metmuseum.org*) or the Smithsonian Institute (*www.smithsonianeducation.org*). Choose one of particular interest to you and write a lesson plan full of ideas about how to engage children or adults in learning more about the exhibit.

Before you get started you might want to investigate some sample lesson plans available at both websites. For examples, go to the Smithsonian website listed above. Search for "lesson plans" and "Franklin" to get to a lesson called Making Friends with Franklin. You will see how the lessons use materials about Benjamin Franklin to teach language arts, science, and visual arts. Or search for lesson plans about "paintings" and look at the lessons about Landscape Painting or Artists Who Love the Land, to teach about the visual arts, American history and culture, American art, geography and maps, world history and culture.

museum visits per year (about 2.3 million visits per day). This all adds up to some very interesting opportunities for museum educators.

Museum educators help people understand the collections of the museum. Their most visible programs include tours for school classes and for the general public. Since no tour can cover every item in the museum, the museum educator selects a representative sample of items, plans an interesting order for the tour, and creates "lesson plans" that tell about each item and its relationship to the whole collection. The educator may create different versions of the tours for different grade levels, for the general public, or for museum members who may have more background in the subject.

Creating and "scripting" the tour is just the beginning of the museum educator's task. The rest of the job includes training staff or volunteers to present the tours; providing background materials for classroom teachers to use before or after the trip; writing, designing, and producing handouts for the public or for school groups; creating tapes for self-guided tours; and putting the educational information on the museum's website. Museum educators may set up workshops, lectures, or film series that relate to an exhibition or to the museum's general mission, and may coordinate any classes, such as studio art and art appreciation that the museum may offer.

Some museum educators specialize in editing and writing, especially the print or on-line magazines the museum may offer to its members. Museum magazines typically feature articles about current exhibits, as well as more general articles about the museum. Editors and writers also create exhibit labels, brochures, and catalogs as well as annual reports, member newsletters, and public relations press releases.

As for job outlook in this field, the U.S. Department of Labor projects that museum jobs are expected to grow as public and private organizations emphasize establishing archives and organizing records and information, and as public interest in science, art, history, and technology increases. And here's a word for the wise: Public interest in smaller, specialized museums with unique collections is expected to increase even faster, so consider becoming an expert in a field you really love and finding a way to share your special knowledge in a special museum.

Search It!
National Teacher Recruitment Clearinghouse at *www. recruitingteachers.org*, American Federation of Teachers–Paraprofessionals and School Related Personnel at *www.aft. org/psrp*, and National Resource Center for Paraprofessionals at *www.nrcpara.org*

Read It!
National Clearinghouse for Paraeducator Resources at *www. usc.edu/dept/education/CMMR/ Clearinghouse.html*

Learn It!
- Minimum of a high school diploma or equivalent
- Two-year associate's degree in child development or early childhood education

Earn It!
Median annual salary is $19,930. (Source: U.S. Department of Labor)

Find It!
Check with your state department of education or the local school district in which you might like to work.

paraprofessional

Paraprofessionals (also known as teacher assistants, paraeducators, and instructional aides) are critical to the success of our schools, particularly at the elementary level. Some paraprofessionals support teachers in totally noninstructional roles. They may be playground or lunchroom attendants, perform clerical tasks such as recording grades and keeping health and attendance records, stocking classroom supplies, and operating audiovisual equipment.

In other situations paraprofessionals take charge of special projects, provide students with individualized, remedial help, and work with special education students or students who do not speak English well. Whatever their assignment, paraprofessionals work for a specific teacher or other edcuational professional who has ultimate responsibility for the design and implementation of educational programs and services.

Paraprofessionals must have very good written and verbal communication skills. They must speak clearly, so students can understand them, and they must speak correctly, because they are serving as role models.

Get Started Now!
- Get experience working with children in the lower grades. If possible, offer to help at a local elementary school or consider assisting adults with scout troops, Sunday school classes, or in after-school child care centers.
- Offer to tutor younger neighbors or relatives with their homework.
- Take elective courses in child development and developmental psychology to broaden your understanding of how to work with children.

Hire Yourself!

You are a paraprofessional in a third grade classroom. Three students in the class have been having difficulty learning their multiplication tables and you have been assigned to work with them. Because they already have anxiety about this area, you have to find fun, game-like activities for them. Check the library for teacher idea books and run Internet searches for "multiplication table lesson plans" or "multiplication table activities" to find at least three appropriate ways to help these students. Do whatever is required to create the materials needed for one of the activities. For instance, this process may involve preparing a set of flash cards or other visual aids.

They must also understand the basics of the subjects they will be working on with the children.

Paraprofessionals fill in the gaps for the classroom teacher who cannot be all things to all students at the same time. They often work with individual students or small groups, giving them the attention, explanations, practice, and reinforcement that will enable them to keep up with the class or have confidence in what they have learned. In middle or high schools, paraprofessionals (like teachers) may specialize in a specific subject area. They may set up equipment for a demonstration in a science class, help students with lab experiments, or give individual attention to students in computer labs. Because paraprofessionals can work with individual students more frequently, they are in a good position to observe performance and evaluate progress of those who have been having difficulty in class. Paraprofessionals often participate in parent conferences to give a more detailed report than the general classroom teacher may be able to do.

Paraprofessionals may also help disabled students with physical needs, such as feeding or grooming, while the teacher continues to work with the rest of the class. As schools continure to integrate special education students into general classrooms, the need for paraprofessionals continues to increase.

Search It!

PE Central at ***www.pecentral.org***

Read It!

PE 4 Life (The "New P.E.") at
www.pe4life.com and
National Association for Sport &
Physical Education (NASPE) at
www.aahperd.org/naspe

Learn It!

Bachelor's degree in health and
physical education.

Earn It!

Median annual salary is $44,267.
(Source: U.S. Department of Labor)

Find It!

Check the department of education
for the state or school district you
are interested in or the Job Center
section at PE Central
(***www.pecentral.org***).

find physical
education
teacher
your future

physical education
teacher

What are your early memories of physical
education (P.E.) classes? Dodgeball? Shooting hoops? Running laps? It
won't be long before your P.E. experience represents the good ol' days
as more schools adopt a new approach known as the "new phys ed" and
gym classes become virtually unrecognizable from the ones you knew.

But what was wrong with the "old" physical education classes, you
ask? For one thing, people who weren't naturally athletic hated them.
And, for many students they didn't just hate the experience; they went
to great lengths to avoid participating in it—a maneuver that puts their
health at risk.

Thanks to the new phys ed, the awful embarrassment often associated with gym class may become a thing of the past. In the new P.E., each
student works toward personal goals and is graded on success in reaching those individualized goals (as opposed to competing with the school
jock for a grade!). Classes focus on strength training, aerobic conditioning, fitness assessment, and stress management to emphasize skills
for maintaining fitness and wellness for life.

Get Started Now!

- Participate in sports such as golf and tennis that can be
  used for lifelong fitness.
- Volunteer to be assistant coach on local teams for soccer,
  baseball, or other sports for children.
- Improve your own total fitness, independent of practice
  for a team sport.

Hire Yourself!

Your new sixth grade P.E. class includes a particularly hard-core group of couch potatoes. You've got to do something to get these kids up and at 'em. Browse around the Centers for Disease Control's "Verb: It's What You Do" website at *www.verbnow.com*. Come up with a plan for using this website to challenge your class to shape up. Make a poster announcing a "Verb" contest that will make it fun for students to get in shape.

The gym of a school that focuses on the new P.E. looks like a health club. Some team sports are still played but students are also lifting weights, using exercise bikes and running machines, rollerblading, and climbing rock walls. Often students wear heart monitors and track the number of minutes they spend with their heartbeat in their target zone.

Physical education teachers must understand human musculoskeletal anatomy including bone, muscle, and neuromuscular structure and their function and application to human movement. They must also be familiar with the care and prevention of athletic injuries. Because they study the various body systems, including major organs and tissues, they are familiar with the body's response to acute and chronic exercise of varying intensity, duration, and frequency.

New phys ed teachers are also trained to accommodate the exceptional learner in regular and special education programs so that students with disabilities have the opportunity to stay fit and healthy as well.

So, because the new P.E. of the future has something for everyone, students can be expected to have a healthier future. This is especially important because studies have found that, on average, only 30 percent of students actually currently participate in P.E., while 70 percent spend most of the class sitting and watching.

All this inactivity is associated with significant health consequences. It is estimated that one out of every four Americans under age 19 is overweight or obese, a figure that has doubled in the past 30 years. Being overweight puts people of all ages at greater risk for a number of preventable and potentially life-threatening diseases.

Of course, changing to the new P.E. requires money for training and for new equipment. The federal government is helping through grants to local school districts and community organizations. The Physical Education for Progress Act provided schools with $5 million in 2001, $40 million in 2002, and $60 million in 2003.

Physical education not only helps physical health, but also seems to help academics and socialization. A study by the California Department of Education, published at the end of 2002, found that at grades five, seven, and nine, students with higher levels of fitness also had higher academic achievement in reading and math. Other school districts have found that the new P.E. creates a more harmonious atmosphere in the school, with less harassment, less bullying, and more respect among students.

Become a physical education teacher and you can help students stay in shape and have fewer diseases for the rest of their lives, help them achieve higher math and reading scores, and reduce violence and bullying in the schools. You may even become one of the most important teachers in your student's lives!

find your
**preschool
teacher**
future

preschool teacher Walk

into a preschool classroom, and you'll see three- and four-year-old children who look like they're having one big play date. All that apparently "aimless" fun is really important, though, since play is the equivalent of an adult's "work." A good preschool experience can lay the foundation for success in the early years of schooling. In fact, a 2003 report issued by the American Federation of Teachers found, like many studies before it, that "quality early childhood education would [among other things] lead to fewer school dropouts and prepare students for productive careers."

As a preschool teacher, you are expected to plan each day's activities, keep records on each child's progress, talk to parents, and think about each child's physical, cognitive (intellectual), emotional, and social growth. It takes a lot of energy to be a preschool teacher! You may not climb, jump, and run as actively as the children do, but you have to be ready to change gears quickly and get to a child who needs you in a hurry. There's no downtime in a preschool teacher's day—preschoolers can't sit patiently while you set up the next activity.

Search It!
National Association for the Education of Young Children at *www.naeyc.org* and Discover The Fun in Learning at *www.preschooleducation.com*

Read It!
Educational Resources Information Center at *http://eric.ed.gov*

Learn It!
- Certification for home-based child care providers
- Associate's or bachelor's degree in early childhood education

Earn It!
Median annual salary is $21,730. (Source: U.S. Department of Labor)

Find It!
Check your local school district to see if there are preschools in nearby public schools. Other preschool programs are run by private individuals, corporations, churches, synagogues, hospitals, colleges, and universities.

Get Started Now!

- Volunteer to work with young children wherever you can—at your place of worship, at community centers, or in after-school programs.
- Read parenting books by a variety of authors. Be aware of the wide range of developmental levels in children of this age.
- Sign up for any child development or early childhood-focused courses at your school.

The preschool teacher may work with individual students, small
groups, or the whole class. After gaining some experience, a preschool
teacher begins to see potential problems in individual children that can be
addressed well before the family might otherwise become aware of them.

Preschool gives children and their families an opportunity to develop positive attitudes about school. A good teacher creates a supportive
environment, where skills and abilities are recognized and where children feel safe to ask for help with the things they can't do. Children who
attend preschool are able to learn the behaviors that will be required to
be successful in elementary school: waiting until you are called upon,
staying with the group during group time, taking turns with equipment,
staying on topic, answering questions, and the concept of consequences
for breaking classroom rules.

Children experience a lot of social growth during the preschool years. At the beginning, many will still be involved in "parallel play," playing next to another child, but not really interacting with him or her. During the course of these years, children learn to play with other individuals, engage in group activities (such as singing, dancing, and games), and share toys and create materials. They learn everyday skills, like putting on a jacket or buttoning a shirt; they form attitudes about the magic of books and the pleasures of art and music; and they use imaginative play to try out adult roles such as mother, father, teacher, or police officer. Preschool activities give children a chance to build their small motor skills, through writing or using scissors; to refine their eye-hand coordination, through throwing and catching games; and to become comfortable with looking at things from left to right, a skill that will be important in reading.

In addition to center-based preschool programs, thousands of people provide child care services in their home. These people are often called child care providers (many do not appreciate being called "baby-sitters") and they care for small groups of children all day while the parents work. Most states require a fairly strict registration and certification process for legally providing this type of child care service.

At this time, most states do not provide adequate access to quality preschool education, and preschool teachers earn significantly less than kindergarten teachers do. However, the American Federation of Teachers and other educational groups are working to change this situation by encouraging policy-makers to implement high standards for preschool programs and increase pay and benefits for preschool teachers.

Search It!
National Association of Elementary School Principals at ***www.naesp.org*** and National Association of Secondary School Principals at ***www.principals.org***

Read It!
Education Week at ***www.educationweek.org*** and Educational Leadership (from the Association for Supervision and Curriculum Development) at ***www.ascd.org***

Learn It!
- Bachelor's degree and teacher certification
- Successful experience as a classroom teacher, athletic coach, or guidance counselor
- Graduate degree in educational administration

Earn It!
Median annual salary is $74,050. (Source: U.S. Department of Labor)

Find It!
View job listings by state by clicking the 'Yellow Pages' icon at ***www.principals.org***.

find your principal future

principal Even though most students (with notable exceptions, of course) share an almost universal dread about getting sent to "the office," disciplining troublemakers is not a principal's primary responsibility. In fact, dealing with problem students accounts for just a small part of a principal's job. The essence of the principal's job is to create an environment where students are physically safe, emotionally secure, and educated to their full potential.

Principals must have strong problem-solving, decision-making, leadership, and team-building skills. They must be big-picture people who can also respond to individual issues with confidence and concern. Principals must know about educational strategies, financial and legal issues affecting schools, administration and organizational management, public relations, and the psychology of groups and individuals.

The school's principal is held accountable for ensuring a high level of education. He or she interviews and hires teachers and other school staff, observes teachers in action, and helps teachers grow in their own professional development. The principal also sets other educational standards, such as how students are grouped into classes, the style of report card to be used, and guidelines for grading students.

The principal's policies affect the general tone of the school: how much emphasis is placed on athletics versus academics; whether the

Get Started Now!
- Get involved in student government to find out more about how your school works behind the scenes.
- Ask your school principal (or a favorite from your elementary or middle school days) for permission to "shadow" him or her for a day to find out what the job is really like. This request would be a natural fit if your school sponsors a "Groundhog Day Job Shadowing" or "Take Your Child to Work" event.

Hire Yourself!

Flash forward 20 years. You've just been hired as principal of the school you now attend. Families in your town are now able to choose the school their children will attend. At an upcoming town meeting, principals from each high school in your district will make a brief presentation about the most distinctive features of their school. Think about your version of a great high school and develop a brochure that describes it well.

Your brochure should include a description of your school, the grade levels it serves, and the basic educational philosophy of the school. Some examples of different philosophical approaches to education include: "magnet schools" for science and technology or music and art or specific career paths; individualized instruction; and an emphasis on team or committee work. Schools may be highly structured or may allow students more choice in what they do to complete course requirements; they may focus more on the "basics" or may focus more on life skills. What will your school be like?

school will position itself as being outstanding in art, science, or some other area; and policies for everything from Internet access to electives. The principal is also responsible for creating and managing the school's budget, reporting test scores to the school board or other supervisors, explaining shortfalls from goals, and developing plans for improving results.

A good principal also nurtures relationships outside of the school itself, creating programs to encourage parent involvement, creating good working relationships with local businesses and community groups, and keeping the school in compliance with all legal requirements. Principals must be aware of and enforce all of the constantly evolving regulations regarding special education, disaster planning, school prayer, and continuing education for teachers.

Principals need to establish, coordinate, and make sure everyone understands emergency responses to a variety of situations. Whether the school is faced with tornado warnings, an earthquake, violence, or a disease epidemic, the principal needs to think quickly, develop and implement a plan, and create an atmosphere of calm and control. Finally, the principal is the person who is charged with communicating to the public—whether the news is good or bad.

Search It!
American Public Health Association
(APHA)at *www.apha.org* and
Society for Public Health Education
(SOPHE) at *www.sophe.org*

Read It!
International Electronic Journal of
Health Education at *www.
aahperd.org/iejhe* and
Centers for Disease Control at
*www.cdc.gov/od/oc/media/
tengpha.htm*

Learn It!
● Bachelor's degree in health education, community health, or
public health
● Master's degree in public health
or health education

Earn It!
Median annual salary is $38,920.
(Source: U.S. Department of Labor)

Find It!
For links to job listings see
www.apha.org/state_ local for
a list of all state public health
associations.

public health educator

Think about this: if you had been born in 1900, you could have expected to live to be 47 years old. On the other hand, a baby born in the year 2000 can expect to live to be 77 years old, an extra 30 years! And if that baby eventually uses seat belts, gets appropriate vaccinations, exercises, and avoids drugs and cigarettes, he or she can expect to live even longer. However, all of the science and medical advances that make this longer life possible would have little or no impact on people's lifestyle choices without public health education and programs.

Public health educators help to prevent disease and promote health by providing people with information and encouraging changes in behavior. Public health educators must be able to communicate information clearly and persuasively, be good listeners and teachers, and be able to work effectively with the different social, cultural, and educational groups within a community. They often have to find ways to overcome barriers of poverty, language, or cultural differences to help

Get Started Now!
● Take classes in biology, chemistry, and behavioral sciences.
● Work on your writing and public speaking skills. Take advantage of opportunities to speak publicly and persuasively, whether it's through a debate team, running for class office, or participating in a fund-raising effort.
● Find out if your school or district offers courses in health care or public health.

everyone take advantage of health care and health education. A public health educator may work in any, or all, of the following settings:

- At corporations and worksites, public health educators may teach workers how to better protect themselves in the workplace. They may teach employees about weight management, smoking cessation, or stress management. Or, they may visit worksites to reach people who might not otherwise know about the health services that are available in the community or about the importance of vaccinations for their children.
- Public health educators in city and state departments of health organize and promote community health programs, such as blood

pressure and cholesterol check-ups, mammograms, and immunizations. In community agencies, they provide information that can reduce the rate of infectious or chronic diseases and promote safety programs such as use of bicycle helmets or child safety seats. Public health educators are often involved in social action for changes in the community. They may evaluate the health education needs of the community, develop new programs, and research the effectiveness of existing ones. They may also train members of the community to educate others in their church, neighborhood, or other groups.

- In private organizations (the American Cancer Society or the March of Dimes, for example) public health educators develop and distribute materials and media campaigns that address issues like disease prevention, detection, and treatment options.
- Public institutions, like schools, libraries, and volunteer organizations, often host classes set up by public health educators to encourage discussion and to teach about prenatal care, substance abuse, and other health and safety issues. They often focus on concerns particular to that area, from earthquake or tornado preparedness to snow shoveling safety, sunburn protection, or prevention of mosquito-borne diseases.
- Public health educators often work with individuals or groups of individuals who share a common concern. They set up programs to help heart attack patients change their eating and exercise behavior or to teach new parents about nutrition and baby care.
- Groups such as the World Health Organization and the Peace Corps employ health educators to direct and coordinate international health work and to educate people about basic health and safety as well as the prevention and control of epidemics and disease.

Given this diverse array of opportunities, aspiring public health educators can expect to find many meaningful ways to make the world a healthier place. Job outlook will remain especially strong if insurance companies continue to emphasize preventive measures and encourage healthy lifestyle choices as a means to contain health care costs.

school media specialist

Search It!
American Library Association at *www.ala.org* and American Association of School Libraries (AASL) at *www.ala.org/ aaslhomeTemplate. cfm?Section=AASL*

In the old, old days, the school librarian was sometimes referred to as the "shush lady." The library was where you went when you really needed to look something up or borrow a book, and the librarian kept reminding you to be really, really quiet while you found what you needed. She would lead you to the card catalog to find a book and then put all the books you looked at back on the shelves in their proper places. Now that we are in the multimedia information age, almost everything about the job has changed, including the title.

Read It!
Teacher Librarian at *www. teacherlibrarian.com*, *Booklist* at *www.ala.org*, and *School Library Journal* at *www.slj.com*

Today's school media specialist is more of a teacher and more a part of the school's educational team than ever before. In elementary and middle schools, whole classes are brought to the media center (formerly known as the library) to get information, to become familiar with print, nonprint, and on-line sources, and most importantly, to acquire the skills needed to find, evaluate, and integrate information from various sources.

Learn It!
● Bachelor's degree with teacher's certification or degree in educational media
● Master's degree in library science

The American Association of School Librarians (AASL) describes the importance of these skills in the parent section of their website: "Learning today means more than memorizing facts. It means learning

Earn It!
Median annual salary is $45,660. (Source: U.S. Department of Labor)

Get Started Now!
● Visit the children's book section of a local library or bookstore to see what kids are reading these days. Do you notice any of your old favorites?
● Find out if your school offers opportunities to assist in the library for elective credit. If so, sign up and find out for yourself what the work is like.
● Broaden your literary horizons by taking as many literature courses as your schedule allows.

Find It!
You can also find many listings at the ALA (*www.ala.org*) and at Library Job Postings on the Internet at *www.libraryjobpostings.org*.

to learn for a lifetime. Savvy parents and educators know that the school library media center is key to teaching students not just to read, but to practice the skills they need to seek, evaluate and use information throughout their lives. In fact, research shows those students from schools with professionally staffed, fully equipped libraries score higher on achievement tests."

The school media specialist must be familiar with the content objectives of each grade and subject area, so that he or she can assemble appropriate reading materials and reference sources. Working with the rest of the school's educational staff, the school media specialist helps to identify the goals of the school's media program, as well as develop policies and practices regarding access to on-line sources, the school's responsibility for filtering objectionable material, and parental involvement.

School media specialists are also responsible for recommending books, magazines, print, and on-line subscriptions and reference materials, and often the actual technological hardware. In fact, in 2002, school media specialists spent more than $1.3 billion on materials that they ordered for their schools. They may also advise the school on which materials to purchase for classroom textbooks and videos, as well as materials for teacher training. With so much money at stake, and with financial resources scarce in individual schools, it is critical that school media specialists be aware of all new instructional materials and order them appropriately. Therefore, much of the school media specialist's time is devoted to reading book reviews and materials from publishers explaining their new products.

find your **school nurse** future

school nurse

Do you remember the school nurse from your elementary or middle school? Many students recall the school nurse as the kindest or most understanding person in their school—the one who was always there to patch up a schoolyard injury, to provide a place to rest, to call a parent for a bad stomachache, and to administer whatever medications students needed to take.

School nurses still take care of big and little emergencies and dispense medications, but their role has grown so much that they are now an integral part of the school team. Of course, school nurses need to be well educated in health information and nursing techniques. Just as importantly, though, they need to really enjoy interacting with students and be compassionate and interested in them. They have to be observant, noticing changes in appearance or behavior. They have to be good administrators, making sure supplies are ordered before they run out and Schedule all the facets of their job. Good school nurses need to stay current on health trends and new ways of handling existing issues. They must be creative teachers, bringing their messages into the classroom, and clear communicators, serving as an intermediary among children, parents, and doctors.

Search It!
National Association of School Nurses at *www.nasn.org*

Read It!
School Nurse Perspectives at *www.homestead.com/snp/ index.html*, School Nurse at *www. schoolnurse.com*, and History of School Nursing at *www.nasn.org/ 100year_AJN_LinaRogers.htm*

Learn It!
Associate's or bachelor's degree in nursing or other health care major.

Earn It!
Average salary for licensed practical nurses is $31,440.
(Source: U.S. Department of Labor)

Find It!
School nursing differs by state and even by county. Nurses may be hired by the school district or by the local health department. There may be a nurse in each school or one for many schools. Check your local school district for details.

Get Started Now!

- Volunteer to work in the school nurse's office in your school. Even if you are just helping with paperwork, you'll have an incredible opportunity to watch how a pro talks to students, parents, and doctors.
- Take first aid classes at your local Red Cross, hospital, or emergency medical center.
- Take classes in science, health, and nutrition.

Hire Yourself!

You have been hired as a school nurse in an elementary school. Make a list of health and safety behaviors you think young children should integrate into their lives, like covering your mouth when you cough and washing your hands often. Make posters for the top five behaviors you want to encourage, using bright colors, clear pictures, and very few words.

Depending on the community, the school nurse may be responsible for any of the following roles:

- Teaching classes. In the younger grades, they might cover basic hygiene, poison prevention, and general safety. In the older grades, school nurses may be responsible for topics as varied as pregnancy prevention, STDs, and child care.
- Educating teachers and administrators. Many children come to school with EpiPens (for emergency allergic reactions), asthma inhalers, and other equipment. School nurses make sure that the responsible adults know how to use these correctly.
- Helping students with special needs. As "mainstreaming" increases and special needs students are no longer isolated in separate schools, it is the school nurse who has to be able to handle (and teach others to handle) things like seizures, testing insulin levels of diabetic students, administering insulin, and even managing feeding tubes and other medical situations.
- Screening for illnesses. School nurses are often the first ones to recognize many conditions, from head lice to sickle cell anemia, eating disorders, nutritional problems, and developmental issues.
- Helping to set school policy. The school nurse helps administrators develop emergency plans for everything from national security alerts to earthquakes, tornadoes, and blizzards.
- Interpreting health-related news for students, parents, and faculty. When the news reports an epidemic (like SARS) or a trend (like keeping anti-radiation pills on hand), the school nurse explains the news and puts it in perspective for the non-medical community.

Nursing is a high-demand profession with opportunities available in almost every city in America. Nursing is also a highly regarded profession which, according to a 2004 Gallup poll, was voted number one for "honesty and ethical standard."

school psychologist

So, exactly what is a school psychologist? School psychologists, guidance counselors, and social workers may all work with individuals or small groups for crisis intervention or prevention, for counseling, and for skill training. But, because they have far more training in psychology, school psychologists focus more on special education students who have identified disabilities and on students who may be facing psychological challenges. They also administer and interpret psycho-educational tests to determine whether a student is eligible for special education services.

A school psychologist may assess preschoolers to see where they should be placed in the school's structure. He or she may work with teachers and parents to cope with a child's developmental delays or help students learn to control their own anxiety and behavior.

School psychologists differ from clinical child psychologists in several ways. For one thing, they are not qualified to open a private practice and work with individual children. On the other hand, they are specialists in learning theory, child development, and mental health and behavior in the school environment.

Working primarily on one or more school campuses allows school psychologists to have direct and sustained access to students. This access often proves critical in helping school psychologists identify students who are dealing with depression, thoughts of suicide, alcohol and

Search It!
National Association of School Psychologists (NASP) at *www. nasponline.org*

Read It!
Student Affiliates of School Psychology: The School Psychologist and SASP News at *www.sasp.addr.com*

Learn It!
- Minimum of a bachelor's degree and completion of a two-year master's program
- Most states now require a specialist degree, which requires an additional year of study

Earn It!
Median annual salary is $56,540. (Source: U.S. Department of Labor)

Find It!
Find jobs for school psychologists at the NASP website (*www. nasponline.org*) and at the Department of Education for your state.

Get Started Now!

- Take child development and psychology courses in school.
- Volunteer for any clubs or committees in your school that involve peer mentoring, peer mediation, or peer support.
- Take a leadership role in any club or activity in which you participate. See if you can communicate clearly, inspire confidence, use critical thinking skills, and solve problems.

substance abuse, dropping out, and family problems. The school psychologist can provide early intervention to coordinate with the child's parents and doctor and address problems before they become too large to address successfully. However, since it is not at all unusual for school psychologists to be assigned to 1,000 or more students, it's important to understand that they generally refer troubled students to other sources for help rather than provide direct therapeutic care themselves.

School psychologists play important roles in helping students deal with the aftermath of traumatic events brought on by natural disasters such as hurricanes, violent acts such as those associated with the 9/11 attacks, and the deaths of classmates or teachers. They often provide workshops for information about important issues such as substance abuse or bullying.

According to the National Clearinghouse for Professions in Special Education, school psychologists are mature, stable and patient, and must be able to maintain professional objectivity when assessing each student's problems and abilities. They must be knowledgeable about various kinds of tests used to measure student's abilities, interests, personality, and achievement.

school social worker

No food for dinner last night, none for breakfast this morning. Mother in the hospital, and no one to take care of the younger kids. Abuse in the family. Not enough money to pay the rent. With so many things going on in so many students' lives, it's no wonder some students can't pay a lot of attention to their class work. School social workers are important in helping students stay healthy, succeed academically, and even stay in school.

The school social worker is the link between the home, the school, and the community. School social workers always have their antennae up for signs of drug or alcohol abuse, eating disorders, teen pregnancy, physical/sexual abuse, or other issues common in the community or age group. They are often the first ones to notice changes in social or academic behavior, increased absences, or other clues that something is "not right" with a child. Students may also initiate contact with the social worker, looking for a safe person to talk to about problems ranging from fighting with a best friend to suicide attempts.

When a school social worker believes a serious problem exists, she may talk to the family at school or in their home, helping parents understand their child's needs. She may refer the child or family to an outside agency or alert a child protection agency to remove the child from a dangerous situation. Sometimes, social workers themselves engage in short-term counseling with individual students or set up a support group of several students facing a common problem, such as a recent divorce in the home.

Get Started Now!
- Volunteer in social service or community support programs.
- Become a peer counselor in your school.
- Follow a solid college prep course of study in high school.

Search It!
School Social Work Association of America (SSWAA) at *www.sswaa.org* and National Association of Social Workers (NASW) at *www.socialworkers.org*

Read It!
Find a variety of articles and resources about social work at *www.socialworkers.org* and *www.cswe.org*

Learn It!
- Master's degree in social work
- Certification as school social work specialist (see *www.socialworkers.org/credentials/specialty/c-ssws.asp*)

Earn It!
Median annual salary is $35,640. (Source: U.S. Department of Labor)

Find It!
Check links to state and regional chapters at the SSWAA website (*www.sswaa.org*) and NASW JobLinks at *http://socialworkers.org/ joblinks/default.asp*.

Hire Yourself!

As a school social worker, you have to be able to elicit information that people may be embarrassed to talk about. For example, a family may not want to admit that they don't have money for food. But, if you know that food is a problem, you can help them fill out forms for free breakfast and lunch at school, tell them about food pantries, and help them get food stamps.

Find out all you can about how someone can access these resources in your community. Use your findings to prepare a resource list you can give to families in need of special food assistance.

School social workers are an integral part of the school community, meeting with teachers and administrators to develop strategies for working with students who have emotional or behavioral problems. They use their knowledge of the "bigger picture" to help teachers better understand the cultural, economic, family, and health issues that contribute to the behavior displayed in the classroom. They also work with the educational team that creates action plans for students with learning disabilities. They support special education teachers in integrating disabled students into the general school population and in making sure laws are followed and paperwork is filed correctly.

School social workers are the contacts at the school for those families who don't know how to help their children. Working with parents who are not well educated themselves or do not speak English well, they help them understand their children's needs and make them aware of the programs available for their children within the school. Social workers can direct families to the appropriate government, community, medical, and social service resources that can help with non-school related issues, such as poverty and illness.

In addition to referring families to the programs that can help them, the school social worker may be the connection between community programs that address common problems such as students dropping out of school or violence in the schools and the students who could benefit from them.

According to the U.S. Department of Labor, employment of school social workers is expected to grow due to expanded efforts to respond to rising student enrollments and increasing numbers of social issues that affect school performance. In addition, continued emphasis on integrating disabled children into the general school population will lead to more jobs in school social work. The need for school social workers is definitely growing; however, availability of state and local funding will ultimately dictate the actual job growth in schools.

find **secondary school** your **teacher** future

Search It!
American Federation of Teachers at *www.aft.org*, National Education Association at *www.nea.org*, and ERIC–The Educational Resources Information Center at *www.eric.ed.gov*

Read It!
Lesson Plans at *www.eduref.org*

Learn It!
- Bachelor's degree, specific teacher training classes, and (usually) student teaching experience
- Successful completion of teaching or subject exam

Earn It!
Median annual salary is $46,010. (Source: U.S. Department of Labor)

Find It!
Visit the Edweek website (*www.agentK-12.org*) and the National Teachers Recruitment Clearinghouse (*www. recruitingteachers.org*).

secondary school teacher

Secondary school teachers have to be experts in the subjects they teach. Just as importantly, they have to be excellent communicators, coaches, and motivators who can get students excited about (or even just tolerant of) those subjects.

Of course, the best experts in a subject are not always the best teachers. Being upbeat and animated goes a long way toward being a good teacher. Knowing how to stay in control of a classroom, consistently searching for creative ways to make the subject exciting, being realistic about what students are capable of at each grade level, and finding the

Get Started Now!
- Learn as much as you can about the subject area you would like to teach.
- See if your school has a Future Educators of America (FEA) chapter. This program, organized by Phi Delta Kappa International (*www.pdkintl.org/studser/fea.htm*), the professional association in education, provides opportunities for middle school and high school students to explore careers in education.
- Check out the teacher associations for the subject areas you are interested in. Some examples of associations include: National Conference of Teachers of English (NCTE) Secondary Home Page: *www.ncte.org/second*; National Science Teachers Association (NSTA): *www.nsta. org*; High School Science Classroom (NSTA): *www.nsta.org/ highschool*; and National Council of Teachers of Mathematics: *www.nctm.org/high*.

Hire Yourself!

A "small school" movement is catching hold in high schools everywhere. Find out why so many schools are incorporating this concept into their schools by reading the latest resources at websites such as the Gates Education Foundation at *www.gatesfoundation.org/Education/SmallHighSchools* and the Small Schools Workshop at *www.smallschoolsworkshop.org*. Use the background information you uncover to compile a chart comparing the pros and cons of small high school programs with the traditionally big high school campus experience.

balance for each class between too easy (boring) and too challenging (frustrating) are other qualities that make some teachers both effective and appreciated by students.

Is high school teaching right for you? Think about teaching situations you have faced in your life. Have you ever tried to explain something to someone and the other person just "didn't get it?" How did you feel? Were you able to remain patient? Did you try different approaches or keep repeating the same thing?

Teaching is a lot more than standing in front of a classroom for 45-minute periods. It includes staying up to date on the subject area and related teaching methods, preparing lessons and projects that will let students discover the subject in their own ways, writing and scoring tests, writing report cards and college recommendations, and taking a sincere interest in your students. Most districts also require teachers to take continuing education classes, which are usually scheduled during those nice long vacations and summer breaks you were looking forward to.

Today there are far more choices in secondary schools than in the past. We have open enrollment policies, where students can apply to go to any school in the district. Federal law also permits students to select a different school if the one assigned to their neighborhood does not meet high standards.

Some high schools are magnet schools or career academies—public schools that focus on a specific area of study (like art and design, performing arts, or technology) or on a specific career area, like health, finance, or public service. Other high schools are "alternative schools," smaller, more flexible public schools that are usually set up for students who have learning disabilities or behavioral problems and need an opportunity to achieve in a different setting.

Search It!
School of Veterinary Medicine–UC Davis at *www.vetmed.ucdavis. edu/CCAB/dogsedu.html* and Assistance Dogs International, Inc. at *www.adionline.org*

Read It!
How Guide Dogs Work at *http://people.howstuffworks. com/guide-dog.htm*, The Puppy Place—So You Want to Be a Guide Dog Trainer? at *www.thepuppyplace.org/ page16.html*, and Delta Society: National Service Dog Center at *www. deltasociety.org/dsb000.htm*

Learn It!
Most animal assistance schools train their own instructors. Some require a college degree.

Earn It!
Average hourly wage is $11. (Source: U.S. Department of Labor)

Find It!
Look on the Internet for jobs available at assistance animal or guide dog facilities.

find your future
service animal instructor

service animal instructor

At some point, you've probably seen a blind person with a guide dog. But did you know that there are many other types of assistance animals that help people with other types of disabilities? And that these animals are not necessarily dogs?

According to the Americans with Disabilities Act, individuals with disabilities may bring their service animals to any public place they choose. According to this law, service animals are individually trained to perform tasks for people with disabilities such as guiding people who are blind, alerting people who are deaf, pulling wheelchairs, or alerting and protecting a person who is having a seizure. Service animals are working animals, not pets.

People in the animal training business usually use the term *assistance animal* to encompass several different types of animals that provide services for the disabled:

- Guide animals help blind and visually impaired individuals navigate traffic, curbs and steps, public transportation, and more.

Get Started Now!

- Spend as much time as possible in animal-training situations. Volunteer to assist an obedience trainer.
- See what it's like to be a guide dog instructor at Guide Dogs for the Blind, Inc. at *www.guidedogs.com/career- leaders.html*.
- Search the Internet for "guide dog schools." Compare different schools in terms of requirements for instructors, length of training for the dog, type of training for the dog, and training for the disabled person.

Hire Yourself!

Use the Internet to seek out resources about a specific disability (like blindness, deafness, or paralysis) of the people who use assistance animals. For each disability, make a chart that defines the disability, lists helpful organizations, and describes at least five ways that an assistance animal might help a person with this type of disability.

While most guide animals are dogs, some schools specialize in training miniature horses to be used for this purpose. Check out the Guide Horse Foundation for the Blind at ***www.guidehorse.com***.

- Hearing dogs serve as the "ears" for deaf and hard of hearing individuals. They are trained to make physical contact with their human partners to alert them to the sounds of a doorbell, telephone, smoke alarm, or alarm clock. Hearing dogs often wear an orange collar and leash or vest in public to identify them as assistance dogs.
- Service animals help the physically disabled with mobility and with many common tasks. They may pull wheelchairs and open and close refrigerators, cabinets, or room doors. They turn lights on and off, retrieve a phone or TV remote control, flush a toilet, make the bed, put clothes in the washer, transfer them to the dryer, and place them in the laundry basket. They can even hand a sales clerk a credit card and take the purchased items in return. Most service animals are dogs, which wear a special backpack or harness when working. Capuchin monkeys are also used as service animals. Check out Helping Hands— Monkey Helpers for the Disabled at ***www. helpinghandsmonkeys.org***.

- Seizure alert dogs are very special service animals. These dogs have the ability to warn a person with epilepsy or other conditions of an impending seizure moments or hours before the clinical signs of a seizure appear. The dog's warning gives the person a chance to get to a safe place or position and minimize the danger of the seizure.

The service animal instructor job has two distinct parts: training the animals and training the people who will partner with those animals. Both require patience, tact, and a sense of humor.

The service animal instructor's work begins after the animal has lived with a "puppy raiser" volunteer and received basic obedience training. The instructor faces several challenges. He or she cannot use food as a reward. The animals must learn to stay focused on their work and not get distracted, even when food is around. The animals also must learn "intelligent disobedience," or when it is critical to not obey a command. For example, an animal that sees a car coming toward it must disobey the command to go. This phase usually takes about six months. When the instructor feels so confident in the animal's training that he or she is willing to be blindfolded and trust the animal under a wide range of circumstances, the animal is paired with its human partner. Training the person and the animal together usually takes four weeks for first-time owners.

Most animal assistant schools train their own instructors through an apprentice system. Some guide dog schools require students to be blindfolded 24 hours a day, for up to 10 days, to experience the training from the clients' point of view. Some teach about basic dog health care and medical and psychological aspects of disabilities.

special education teacher

Want a teaching job that is a real challenge, incredibly rewarding, allows you to be creative in developing specialized programs for each child's individual needs, and is never, ever routine or boring? Want the opportunity to develop meaningful relationships with your students? Special education may be the place for you!

Since early intervention is the most effective way to reach children with disabilities, many special education teachers work with infants and toddlers in the child's own home. Others work in hospitals, residential facilities, and medical centers. Their students may be infants, school children, or adults. However, the great majority of special ed teachers work in schools.

Traditionally, schools placed children with disabilities in self-contained classrooms. A student who demonstrated the ability to keep up with the work was then "mainstreamed" into one or more "regular" classes. Many schools now operate on an "inclusion" model, where, to the greatest degree possible, students are placed in the class they would

Get Started Now!

- Volunteer to work at a hospital, rehab center, or other facility for children with disabilities.
- Put yourself in situations where you can evaluate your own patience, acceptance of others, flexibility, and creativity. Whether it's training animals or giving music lessons, you'll be able to see if you have the personality this career needs.
- Take courses in early childhood development and developmental psychology.

Search It!
Council for Exceptional Children (CEC) at *www.cec.sped.org* and National Clearinghouse for Professions in Special Education (NCPSE) at *www.special-ed-careers.org*

Read It!
National Information Center for Children and Youth with Disabilities (NICHCY) at *www.nichcy.org*, IDEA Practices at *www.ideapractices.org*, and Teachers Helping Teachers at *www.pacificnet.net/~mandel/SpecialEducation.html*

Learn It!
- Bachelor's degree in special education
- Master's degree a plus for advancement in the field

Earn It!
Median annual salary is $45,510. (Source: U.S. Department of Labor)

Find It!
Both of the organizations listed above (CEC and NCPSE) maintain a large database of available jobs.

Hire Yourself!

Obtain one of the books or movies listed below at your local library. Read it or watch it and write a one page summary telling how the "special needs" person featured in the story was helped or let down by the schools or the general community where he or she lived.

Sample books include:

- *Buster and the Amazing Daisy*: *Adventures with Asperger Syndrome,* by Nancy Ogaz (Philadelphia: Jessica Kingsley Publishers, 2002)
- *My Name is Brian Brain,* by Jeanne Betancourt (New York: Scholastic, 2001)
- *Freak the Mighty,* by Rodman Philbrick (New York: Scholastic, 2001)
- *Educating Tigers,* by Wendy Sand Eckel (Frederick, Md.: PublishAmerica, 2000)

Or look for these classic movies at your local library or video rental store: *Rainman, Charly, Children of a Lesser God,* and *The Miracle Worker.*

normally be assigned to. The goal is for the student to be able to benefit from being in the class. There is no requirement that he/she be able to keep up with the other students. The "full inclusion" model calls for all students, regardless of handicapping condition or severity, to be in a regular classroom full time.

When a school has an inclusion policy, special education teachers may work in resource rooms, special areas where individual students or small groups can come for part of the day. Special ed teachers also work alongside the classroom teacher to help adapt lessons to the special needs child and to work with those students individually.

Students in special education programs represent a wide range of abilities and needs. Some have specific learning disabilities, emotional disturbances, speech or language difficulties, or mental retardation. Others have physical disabilities, including hearing and vision impairments or problems with motor skills.

Another major component of the special education teacher's job is observing and evaluating students to determine their needs. In fact, it is sometimes the special education teacher who first identifies a student's limitations or special needs. Special education teachers are also program planners, evaluating curriculum and modifying lesson plans or developing new ones. They may adapt standard learning materials or

design more appropriate tools. Special education is a people job, but it also includes a substantial amount of paperwork. To fulfill legal requirements, teachers must document the programs developed for each student as well as the student's progress.

Most importantly, the special education teacher is a part of the child's educational team, working with school administration, parents, classroom teachers, and counselors to develop and implement an individualized education program (IEP) for each student and keeping communication lines open among all members of the team.

Search It!

The American Speech-Language-Hearing Association (ASHA) at *www.asha.org* and National Student Speech Language Hearing Association (NSSLHA) at *www.nsslha.org*

Read It!

Friends: The Association of Young People Who Stutter at *www.friendswhostutter.org*, National Stuttering Association (NSA) at *www.nsastutter.org*, and National Aphasia Association at *www.aphasia.org*

Learn It!

- Forty-five states require a master's degree and licensing for speech-language pathologists
- Continuing education is usually required for license renewal

Earn It!

Median annual salary is $49,450. (Source: U.S. Department of Labor)

Find It!

Find out about speech pathologist jobs and resources at *www.speechpathologist.org*.

speech-language pathologist

Former President Gerald Ford once said, "Nothing in life is more important than the ability to communicate effectively." Language and communication skills are essential in school, in social settings, and on the job.

Speech-language pathologists (also known as speech therapists) assess, diagnose, and treat problems with speech and language, as well as difficulties with swallowing. At least 14 million Americans, almost half of them under the age of 18, have speech, voice, or language disorders.

Professionally speaking, speech and language are definitely not the same thing. Language has to do with the "rules" of communicating. It includes things like what individual words mean, how to make new words (for example: happy, happier, happiest, happily), and how to put words together to express a thought. While we say, "The baby was happy with the red truck," someone with a language disorder might instead say, "Truck red the happy baby was." Some people with language problems can understand speech, but cannot convey ideas to others. Others may speak, but cannot comprehend.

Get Started Now!

- Ask your guidance counselor or teacher to help arrange a visit with your school district's speech-language pathologist to find out more about what the job is really like.
- Do volunteer work with young children—test your ability to be patient, tolerant, resourceful, and creative.
- Study a foreign language or take a linguistics course to broaden your awareness of how words are used to communicate ideas and emotions.

Hire Yourself!

You just started working as a speech-language patholo-gist in an elementary school. A teacher has referred a second grade student who stutters to you for help. Use resources such as those found on-line at *www.stuttering.net* and elsewhere to find five activities to use with the student. Prepare a written lesson plan that outlines how to incorpo-rate each activity into your first therapy session.

Speech-language pathologists in schools play a critical role by screening young children for delayed language and language disorders and then beginning immediate intervention. According to the American Speech-Language-Hearing Association, children who have problems with spoken language often have difficulty in learning to read and write, and children with reading and writing problems are often found to have problems using language to communicate, think, and learn. When language problems are identified and addressed quickly, these children can be much more successful in reading and writing. Other language problems common in children and adolescents include difficulty with giving and understanding directions, with using grammar correctly, and with using language that is appropriate to a social situation.

Speech, unlike language, refers to making the correct sounds in the correct places. Problems include stuttering, garbled sounds, and voices that sound rough, hoarse, monotone, or nasal.

Children (and adults) who stutter can make their speech more fluent and cope with their disorder through the intervention of a speech-language pathologist. Individuals who cannot produce certain sounds correctly (lisping, for example) can learn to produce those sounds more clearly, and those with poor voice quality can learn to better control their vocal and respiratory systems.

Speech-language pathologists are important to older people as well as to children. Speech-language professionals can help people with aphasia (a loss of speech and language abilities) caused by a stroke, brain trauma, or cancer to regain lost speech and language abilities.

Many speech-language pathologists choose to specialize in communications in a business environment, including helping businesspeople reduce or modify a foreign or regional accent. Speech-language pathologists do not promote eliminating all regional accents, but there are times when the accent itself, rather than the content of what is being said, becomes the focus of people's attention, and the person and his company become less productive. Voice training is often requested for the same reason. Public speaking and presentation training can make all the difference in how people perceive an individual's work, as can non-verbal communication, learning how to recognize and use the messages conveyed by gesture, facial expression, and body postures and in communication etiquette.

In whatever situation speech-language pathologists choose to work, it is critical that they become very familiar with the cultural, verbal, and non-verbal traditions of the people they are working with. If you say "tomato," and your client says "tomahto," or you say "Harvard," and your client says "Hahvahd," your client does not necessarily need therapy. It all depends on where you and your client live. Similarly, a child might mistakenly be referred for speech-language therapy by a professional who is unaware that, in that child's native culture, children are expected to address adults in a low voice and without making eye contact.

The U.S. Department of Labor projects that employment of speech-language pathologists and audiologists is expected to grow faster than the average for all occupations through the year 2012. This is true due to a variety of factors including a rapidly growing population of people who are over the age of 55, who are more likely to need speech-language services due to medical conditions; medical advances that improve the survival rates of premature infants and stroke victims; and growth in elementary and secondary school enrollments.

Search It!

National Association of Student Personnel Administrators at *www.naspa.org*, National Academic Advising Association at *www.nacada.ksu.edu*, and National Association of Financial Aid Administrators at *www.nasfaa.org*

student affairs officer

Some colleges and universities develop their strong reputations from the activities of their teaching faculty, others from their research facilities or their athletic programs. The one thing that all institutions of higher education do have in common is dedicated student affairs professionals who make the school a comfortable and livable place for students.

There are many different areas of student affairs, and schools often group and label those areas in different ways. However, the major function of this department can be summarized as providing counseling, management, and administration of all aspects of campus life outside of the classroom. The specialized functions may include any combination of the following:

- Admissions counselors recruit students who will best fit at the institution, encourage them to apply, and then makes decisions on who to accept out of all the applications received. Many schools have recently introduced the position of enrollment manager, whose job is to identify those applicants who are most likely to stay at the school and graduate from it. A very strong candidate who drops out to start his own business or join a professional

Read It!

NetResults at *www.naspa.org/netresults* and Student Affairs On-Line at *www.studentaffairs.com/ejournal*

Learn It!
- Bachelor's degree required for junior positions
- Master's degree required for more advanced positions

Earn It!

Median annual salary is $41,050. (Source: U.S. Department of Labor)

Find It!

Check out job opportunities in student affairs at *www.studentaffairs.com* and National Association of Student Personnel Administrators at *www.naspa.org*.

Get Started Now!
- Get involved in organizing your school's after-school activities whether it's decorating for the prom or painting sets for the next drama production.
- Make a habit of using a daily calendar to keep track of your activities.
- Check out the student affairs sections found at the websites of a variety of colleges.

Hire Yourself!

You have just been selected as orientation advisor for a large university. Make a list of your goals for orientation—what should students come away with after this period? Hint: it's more than just phone numbers of potential dates and a list of which teachers give the easiest grades! What activities can you design that will achieve those goals? You may want to get ideas from the National Orientation Directors Association (*www.nodaweb.org*). How would you recruit current students to work in the new student orientation? What is your idea of an ideal mix of special interest dorms? Why do you think this mix would be a good one?

sports team is not as good for the school as someone who will be part of the school for four years and become a successful alumnus.

- Campus activities and student organization specialists provide opportunities for students to develop leadership and organizational skills. Counselors in this area may also oversee fraternities, sororities, and other organizations on campus.

- Financial aid counselors are experts in their knowledge of federal, state, and local programs and regulations. They recommend strategies for obtaining financial aid and help students put together the aid package that is most appropriate for each individual.

- Career services personnel may use counseling and/or testing to help students decide on a career path, help them find part-time or summer employment, and arrange for on-campus recruiting by major employers.

- Counseling deans or directors in the student affairs area oversee various counseling professionals on campus who are available to help students with personal and academic problems.

- Residence life staff deal with some of the high profile issues of campus life. Student residence plans have become major issues for discussion and protest on many campuses. Residence life professionals determine policies such as whether freshmen will be isolated or integrated with other students and whether dorms should be heterogeneous or set up as special ethnic or interest groups. They also set policies for the smooth functioning of the campus residence facilities.

- Student orientation programs are designed by professionals in the student affairs office to help entering students succeed at the school both socially and academically. Many schools now offer orientation programs that continue throughout the students' first year.
- Student union or student center professionals make and implement decisions about what facilities will be available, what retail services will be provided, and what outside speakers will be brought to the school.
- Other student affairs services may be provided to support and advocate for specific groups of students, such as students with disabilities, veterans, women, alumni, or international students.

Since student affairs officers set the tone for virtually every aspect of campus life, they must conduct themselves in ways that reflect positively on the college. Those hired for these positions generally have at least a bachelor's degree, exceptional interpersonal skills, and a genuine interest in helping others succeed.

studio animal trainer

Animals definitely add an extra dimension to movies, whether it's the owls, cats, toads, and rats helping Harry Potter, the army of hamsters overrunning the campus of the Nutty Professor, or Babe the pig and his various friends. Way before *Animal Planet* ever existed, TV animals were crucial to the success of many shows and to commercials pitching everything from pet food to cars and trucks.

A dedicated group of well-prepared trainers and a talented collection of animals work long and hard to make these movies possible. And there are more trainers and animals used for every scene than you would ever predict!

In most films, roles that appear to be played by one animal are actually played by many. In the first Harry Potter movie, Hedwig, Harry's personal owl, was actually played by seven different owls. And the role of Scabbers, Ron Weasley's fat rat, was shared by 12 different real rats, plus one mechanical rat. Remember Fang, Hagrid's loyal companion? It took four Neapolitan Mastiffs to get that character on screen. As for the number of animal trainers in a movie, each of the owls in the Harry Potter film had at least one trainer on the set.

Studio animal trainers need to be able to sustain long hours, crouch in uncomfortable positions to stay out of camera range, do some heavy lifting, and other physical work. And remember—animals still need the same care on weekends and holidays. This career is a lifestyle, not just a job!

Get Started Now!

- Spend as much time with animals as you can. Volunteer with a veterinarian, shelter, nature center, or zoo.
- Work on oral presentation skills that you will need for education programs.

Hire Yourself!

Go on-line to the American Humane Association site (*www.ahafilm.org/reviews.html*). Read the reviews of three films listed on this website. Create a chart comparing the types of animals featured in each film and the tasks they performed. Use a highlighter to indicate the three tasks that you think would be the most fun to train an animal to do.

Trainers who work with animals that are not typical house pets can also use their skills to help educate children and adults. In the new zoos and aquariums, often called wildlife conservation parks, zookeepers no longer just feed, water, and clean the shelters of their animals. They are now responsible for keeping the animals healthy (physically and mentally), helping them breed in captivity, and developing exhibits, presentations, and performances that help the public understand and appreciate these animals and support their conservation.

Trainers, whose main function is to modify animal behavior, also help zoos manage the animals and keep them healthy. When animals are trained to enter chutes or crates in response to trainers' commands and rewards, caretakers are able to take blood or urine samples, give vaccinations, treat wounds, and perform other minor procedures without the need for chemical or physical restraints. Some animals have been trained to open their mouths for exams or present various body parts to the cage mesh, allowing keepers and veterinarians to examine them more frequently and without using restraints.

Other benefits of training animals include giving them the kind of mental and physical challenges that they would experience in the wild and minimizing some behavior (like aggression) by teaching different animals to feed at different places.

teacher of the visually impaired

teacher of the visually impaired

Search It!
American Foundation for the Blind at *www.afb.org* and Association for Education and Rehabilitation of the Blind and Visually Impaired at *www.aerbvi.org*

Read It!
National Federation of the Blind at *www.nfb.org/kids.htm*, Future Reflections at *www. nfb.org/futref.htm*, and Orientation and Mobility in the Public Schools at *www. wayfinding.net/publcsch.htm*

Learn It!
● Bachelor's degree in special education
● Graduate degree in teaching or in orientation and mobility

Earn It!
Median annual salary is $42,690. (Source: U.S. Department of Labor)

Find It!
Find employment opportunities at The Special Education Exchange at *www.spedex.com/jobs/jobs. htm* or at your school district website.

teacher of the visually impaired

Did you know that up to 80 percent of everything we learn in our first three years is learned through the use of vision? Babies learn to do most things by imitation—whether it's playing with a toy, feeding themselves, or even giving a hug or a kiss. At an early age, they learn to read emotions, relying heavily on facial expressions and body language, in addition to tone of voice.

Without vision, an infant has no motivation to hold his head up—and therefore doesn't develop the strong neck and shoulder muscles needed for standing and walking. Without vision, the toddler does not feel the need to crawl, and eventually walk, towards things. For children who

Get Started Now!

● Simulate what it's like for people with different low-vision conditions. Go to the website of the Ohio Lions Club Eye Research (*www.ohiolionseyeresearch.com*), and click on "simulations."
● Check into the availability of Braille courses offered through your community's continuing education program.
● Go to the websites for the schools for the blind shown on the website *www.ncecbvi.org/schlist.html*. Find two schools that you would especially like to work at and write down what it is about those schools that most appeals to you.
● Find out how your name is spelled in Braille at *www. hotbraille.com*.
● Learn more about how vision works at *http://science. howstuffworks.com/eye1.htm*

126

Hire Yourself!

You've been hired to open a resource center for visually impaired people in your area. Look at some of the special products offered for blind and low vision adults and children. Which would you stock in your center? Hint: two excellent catalogs of products are MaxiAids at *www.maxiaids.com* and LSS Products at *www. lssproducts.com*. Make your own catalog of the 25 products you recommend purchasing first.

are born blind or with extremely limited vision, it is therefore critical to identify and address the situation at the earliest possible age.

Teachers of the visually impaired (or VI teachers) work directly with children who have vision problems. Even more importantly, they work with the children's parents to show them what they can do to help their child keep up developmentally with sighted children. While the parents need an opportunity to work through their own feelings about their child's blindness, they also need to learn about how it can affect their child's intellectual, motor, and social development.

By preschool, many visually impaired children can attend school with sighted classmates, especially if the classroom teacher works closely with the VI teacher. Orientation and mobility (O&M) specialists also work with the child to teach him to navigate safely and independently in his environment.

During the school year, the VI teacher works with the classroom teacher and the student to ensure that the student receives everything that sighted students receive (such as Braille report cards), to help adapt lessons (such as using an abacus for math), and to help the student learn appropriate social skills.

When working with adults, O&M specialists teach clients life skills (like coding clothes by color, handling money, and working in the kitchen), as well as more specific navigational skills (route planning, compass direction, cane techniques, public transportation, crossing streets, traffic control devices, and indoor navigation for malls, store, and homes). They also help clients with body image and orientation within the environment, as well as motor skills for balance and posture and social skills (such as restaurant dining). O&M specialists need to be familiar with all of the devices available for the blind and visually impaired and provide training in how to use them.

do you have the right skills?

Career exploration is, in one sense, career matchmaking. The goal is to match your basic traits, interests and strengths, work values, and work personality with viable career options.

But the "stuff" you bring to a job is only half of the story.

Choosing an ideal job and landing your dream job is a two-way street. Potential employers look for candidates with specific types of skills and backgrounds. This is especially true in our technology-infused, global economy.

In order to find the perfect fit, you need to be fully aware of not only what you've got, but also what prospective employers need.

The following activity is designed to help you accomplish just that. This time we'll use the "wannabe" approach —working with careers you think you want to consider. This same matchmaking process will come in handy when it comes time for the real thing too.

Unfortunately, this isn't one of those "please turn to the end of the chapter and you'll find all the answers" types of activities. This one requires the best critical thinking, problem-solving, and decision-making skills you can muster.

Big Activity #5:
do you have the right skills?

Here's how it works:

Step 1: First, make a chart like the one on page 130.

Step 2: Next, pick a career profile that interests you and use the following resources to compile a list of the traits and skills needed to be successful. Include:

- Information featured in the career profile in this book;
- Information you discover when you look through websites of any of the professional associations or other resources listed with each career profile;
- Information from the career profiles and skills lists found on-line at America's Career InfoNet at *www.acinet.org*.

Briefly list the traits or skills you find on separate lines in the first column of your chart.

Step 3: Evaluate yourself as honestly as possible. If, after careful consideration, you conclude that you already possess one of the traits or skills included on your list, place an *X* in the column marked "Got It!" If you conclude that the skill or trait is one you've yet to acquire, follow these directions to complete the column marked "Get It!":

- If you believe that gaining proficiency in a skill is just a matter of time and experience and you're willing to do whatever it takes to acquire that skill, place a *Y* (for yes) in the corresponding space.
- Or, if you are quite certain that a particular skill is one that you don't possess now, and either can't or won't do what it takes to acquire it, mark the corresponding space with an *N* (for no). For example, you want to be a brain surgeon. It's important, prestigious work and the pay is good. But, truth be told, you'd rather have brain surgery yourself than sit through eight more years of really intense science and math. This rather significant factor may or may not affect your ultimate career choice. But it's better to think it through now rather than six years into med school.

Step 4: Place your completed chart in your Big Question AnswerBook.

When you work through this process carefully, you should get some eye-opening insights into the kinds of careers that are right for you. Half reality check and half wake-up call, this activity lets you see how you measure up against important workforce competencies.

Big Activity #5: **do you have the right skills?**

skill or trait required	got it!	get it!

more career ideas in education and training

Careers featured in the previous section represent mainstream, high-ly viable occupations where someone with the right set of skills and training stands more than half a chance of finding gainful employ-ment. However, these ideas are just the beginning. There are lots of ways to make a living in any industry—and this one is no exception.

Following is a list of career ideas related in one way or another to education and training. This list is included here for two reasons. First, to illustrate some unique ways to blend your interests with opportuni-ties. Second, to keep you thinking beyond the obvious.

As you peruse the list you're sure to encounter some occupations you've never heard of before. Good. We hope you get curious enough to look them up. Others may trigger one of those "aha" moments where everything clicks and you know you're onto something good. Either way we hope it helps point the way toward some rewarding opportuni-ties in the fields of education and training.

Admissions Counselor

Adult Literacy and Remedial
Education Specialist

Archivist

Art Teacher

Art Therapist

Athletic Trainer

Audiovisual Technician

Bookmobile Coordinator

Buildings and Grounds
Maintenance Worker

Business Teacher

Cafeteria Cook

Campus Monitor

Child Care Provider

Childbirth Educator

College President

Community College
Instructor

Curator

Custodian

Dance Teacher

Dean

Dietician

Drama Teacher

Driving Instructor

Early Childhood
Program Director

Educational Diagnostician

Educational Researcher

English Teacher

Flight Instructor

Food Service Manager

Grant Writer

Historical Interpreter

Instructional Media Designer

Instructional Supervisor

Instructional Technology
Specialist

K9 Police Dog Trainer

Kindergarten Teacher

Library Assistant

Medical Writer

Music Writer

Nutritionist

Occupational Therapist

Personnel Administrator

Provost

Reading Specialist

Registrar

School Bus Driver

School Business Manager

School Resource Officer

School Secretary

School Security Officer

School Superintendent

Special Education Teacher

Sports Instructor

Substitute Teacher

Textbook Editor

Transportation Coordinator

Vocational Rehabilitation
Counselor

Big Question #6:
are you on the right path?

You've covered a lot of ground so far. You've had a chance to discover more about your own potential and expectations. You've taken some time to explore the realities of a wide variety of career opportunities within this industry.

Now, is a good time to sort through all the details and figure out what all this means to you. This process involves equal measures of input from your head and your heart. Be honest, think big, and, most of all, stay true to you.

You may be considering an occupation that requires years of advanced schooling which, from your point of view, seems an insurmountable hurdle. What do you do? Give up before you even get started? We hope not. We'd suggest that you try some creative thinking.

Big Activity #6:
are you on the right path?

Start by asking yourself if you want to pursue this particular career so badly that you're willing to do whatever it takes to make it. Then stretch your thinking a little to consider alternative routes, nontraditional career paths, and other equally meaningful occupations.

Following are some prompts to help you sort through your ideas. Simply jot down each prompt on a separate sheet of notebook paper and leave plenty of space for your responses.

Big Activity #6: **are you on the right path?**

One thing I know for sure about my future occupation is

I'd prefer to pursue a career that offers

I'd prefer to pursue a career that requires

A career option I'm now considering is

What appeals to me most about this career is

What concerns me most about this career is

Things that I still need to learn about this career include

Big Activity #6: are you on the right path?

Another career option I'm considering is

What appeals to me most about this career is

What concerns me most about this career is

Things that I still need to learn about this career include

Of these two career options I've named, the one that best fits most of my interests, skills, values, and work personality is   because

At this point in the process, I am

❑ Pretty sure I'm on the right track

❑ Not quite sure yet but still interested in exploring some more

❑ Completely clueless about what I want to do

SECTION 3
experiment with success

Right about now you may find it encouraging to learn that the average person changes careers five to seven times in his or her life. Plus, most college students change majors several times. Even people who are totally set on what they want to do often end up being happier doing something just a little bit different from what they first imagined.

So, whether you think you've found the ultimate answer to career happiness or you're just as confused as ever, you're in good company. The best advice for navigating these important life choices is this: Always keep the door open to new ideas.

As smart and dedicated as you may be, you just can't predict the future. Some of the most successful professionals in any imaginable field could never ever have predicted what—and how—they would be doing what they actually do today. Why? Because when they were in high school those jobs didn't even exist. It was not too long ago that there were no such things as personal computers, Internet research, digital cameras, mass e-mails, cell phones, or any of the other newfangled tools that are so critical to so many jobs today.

Keeping the door open means being open to recognizing changes in yourself as you mature and being open to changes in the way the world works. It also involves a certain willingness to learn new things and tackle new challenges.

It's easy to see how being open to change can sometimes allow you to go further in your chosen career than you ever dreamed. For instance, in almost any profession you can imagine, technology has fueled unprecedented opportunities. Those people and companies who have embraced this "new way of working" have often surpassed their original expectations of success. Just ask Bill Gates. He's now one of the world's wealthiest men thanks to a company called Microsoft that he cofounded while still a student at Harvard University.

It's a little harder to see, but being open to change can also mean that you may have to let go of your first dream and find a more appropriate one. Maybe your dream is to become a professional athlete. At this point in your life you may think that there's nothing in the world that would possibly make you happier. Maybe you're right and maybe you have the talent and persistence (and the lucky breaks) to take you all the way.

But maybe you don't. Perhaps if you opened yourself to new ideas you'd discover that the best career involves blending your interest in sports with your talent in writing to become a sports journalist or sports information director. Maybe your love of a particular sport and your interest in working with children might best be served in a coaching career. Who knows what you might achieve when you open yourself to all the possibilities?

So, whether you've settled on a career direction or you are still not sure where you want to go, there are several "next steps" to consider. In this section, you'll find three more Big Questions to help keep your career planning moving forward. These Big Questions are:

❓ Big Question #7: **who knows what you need to know?**

❓ Big Question #8: **how can you find out what a career is really like?**

❓ Big Question #9: **how do you know when you've made the right choice?**

Big Question #7:
who knows what you need to know?

When it comes to the nitty-gritty details about what a particular job is really like, who knows what you need to know? Someone with a job like the one you want, of course. They'll have the inside scoop—important information you may never find in books or websites. So make talking to as many people as you can part of your career planning process.

Learn from them how they turned their own challenges into opportunities, how they got started, and how they made it to where they are now. Ask the questions that aren't covered in "official" resources, such as what it is really like to do their job, how they manage to do a good job and have a great life, how they learned what they needed to learn to do their job well, and the best companies or situations to start in.

A good place to start with these career chats or "informational interviews" is with people you know—or more likely, people you know who know people with jobs you find interesting. People you already know include your parents (of course), relatives, neighbors, friends' parents, people who belong to your place of worship or club, and so on.

All it takes to get the process going is gathering up all your nerve and asking these people for help. You'll find that nine and a half times out of 10, the people you encounter will be delighted to help, either by providing information about their careers or by introducing you to people they know who can help.

hints and tips for a successful interview

● TIP #1

Think about your goals for the interview, and write them down.

Be clear about what you want to know after the interview that you didn't know before it.

Remember that the questions for all personal interviews are not the same. You would probably use different questions to write a biography of the person, to evaluate him or her for a job, to do a history of the industry, or to learn about careers that might interest you.

Writing down your objectives will help you stay focused.

● TIP #2

Pay attention to how you phrase your questions.

Some questions that we ask people are "closed" questions; we are looking for a clear answer, not an elaboration. "What time does the movie start?" is a good example of a closed question.

Sometimes, when we ask a closed question, we shortchange ourselves. Think about the difference between "What times are the showings tonight?" and "Is there a 9 P.M. showing?" By asking the second question, you may not find out if there is an 8:45 or 9:30 show.

That can be frustrating. It usually seems so obvious when we ask a question that we expect a full answer. It's important to remember, though, that the person hearing the question doesn't always have the same priorities or know why the question is being asked.

The best example of this? Think of the toddler who answers the phone. When the caller asks, "Is your mom home?" the toddler says, "Yes" and promptly hangs up. Did the child answer the question? As far as he's concerned, he did a great job!

Another problem with closed questions is that they sometimes require so many follow-up questions that the person being interviewed feels like a suspect in an interrogation room.

A series of closed questions may go this way:

Q: What is your job title?
A: Assistant Producer
Q: How long have you had that title?
A: About two years.

Q: What was your title before that?
Q: How long did you have that title?
Q: What is the difference between the two jobs?
Q: What did you do before that?
Q: Where did you learn to do this job?
Q: How did you advance from one job to the next?

An alternative, "open" question invites conversation. An open-question interview might begin this way:

I understand you are an Assistant Producer. I'm really interested in what that job is all about and how you got to be at the level you are today.

Open questions often begin with words like:

Tell me about . . .
How do you feel about . . .
What was it like . . .

● TIP #3

Make the person feel comfortable answering truthfully.
In general, people don't want to say things that they think will make them look bad. How to get at the truth? Be empathic, and make their answers seem "normal."

Ask a performer or artist how he or she feels about getting a bad review from the critics, and you are unlikely to hear, "It really hurts. Sometimes I just want to cry and get out of the business." Or "Critics are so stupid. They never understand what I am trying to do."

Try this approach instead: "So many people in your industry find it hard to deal with the hurt of a bad critical review. How do you handle it when that happens?"

ask the experts

You can learn a lot by interviewing people who are already successful in the types of careers you're interested in. In fact, we followed our own advice and interviewed several people who have been successful in the fields of education and training to share with you here.

Before you get started on your own interview, take a few minutes to look through the results of some of ours. To make it easier for you to compare the responses of all the people we interviewed, we have presented our interviews as a panel discussion that reveals important "success" lessons these people have learned along the way. Each panelist is introduced on the next page.

Our interviewees gave us great information about things like what their jobs are really like, how they got to where they are, and even provided a bit of sage advice for people like you who are just getting started.

So Glad You Asked

In addition to the questions we asked in the interviews in this book, you might want to add some of these questions to your own interviews:

- How did your childhood interests relate to your choice of career path?
- How did you first learn about the job you have today?
- In what ways is your job different from how you expected it to be?
- Tell me about the parts of your job that you really like.
- If you could get someone to take over part of your job for you, what aspect would you most like to give up?
- If anything were possible, how would you change your job description?
- What kinds of people do you usually meet in your work?
- Walk me through the whole process of getting your type of product made and distributed. Tell me about all the people who are involved.
- Tell me about the changes you have seen in your industry over the years. What do you see as the future of the industry?
- Are there things you would do differently in your career if you could do it all over?

real people with real jobs in education and training

Following are introductions to our panel of experts. Get acquainted with their backgrounds and then use their job titles to track their stories throughout the seven success lessons.

- **Nursery School Teacher Mary Belkin** lives and teaches in Hastings-on-Hudson, New York.
- **BJ Berquist** is an **Art Teacher** who works in a juvenile correctional facility in Loysville, Pennsylvania.
- **Chris Bowser** works as the **Education Director** of the Hudson River Sloop Clearwater project, a nonprofit organization in Poughkeepsie, New York.
- **Carol Carter** is an author, a **College/Career Advisor**, and president of Lifebound, a life and career coaching company in Denver, Colorado.
- **Anna Beth Crabtree** is **Director of Library Services** for St. John's Health System in Springfield, Missouri.
- **Dr. William Howe** is an **Educational Consultant** who specializes in multicultural education and gender equality issues for the Connecticut State Department of Education.
- **Barbara Klipper** works as a **Librarian** in Stamford, Connecticut.
- **Roger Lazoff** is a **Museum Educator** for the South Street Seaport Museum in New York, New York.
- **George Megrue, Ph.D.** works for the Ridgefield Board of Education in Ridgefield, Connecticut, as a **Middle School Counselor**.
- **Robert Roberge** is a **Personal Trainer and Nutritionist** and works at the Kneaded Touch in Stamford, Connecticut.
- **Linda Ilene Slone** is a **Speech-Language Pathologist** in Palo Alto, California.
- **Lisa Wright** is a **Teacher of the Visually Impaired** for Anne Arundel County Public Schools in Annapolis, Maryland.

Mary Belkin

Carol Carter

Dr. William Howe

Barbara Klipper

Robert Roberge

Work is a good thing when you find the right career.

● **Tell us what it's like to work in your current career.**

Teacher of the Visually Impaired: As an itinerant teacher of the visually impaired I work with children of all ages—birth through 21 at many different schools. The job has a lot of variety, keeps you moving all day, gives you the opportunity to work with children of different ages, different abilities, and teach a variety of skills. It is definitely not boring! Some people may not like the instability of not working at one school, but I love it.

Director of Library Services: My job involves managing library services and two libraries for a large regional health care organization that employs over 7,200 people. I am responsible for developing the collections; providing health information and library services to health professionals, employees, patients, family members and community residents; marketing and library promotion; managing the budget; writing grants; and teaching computer and library-related courses.

Personal Trainer/Nutritionist: Being a good personal trainer is much more difficult than most would imagine. It requires a great deal of focus and concentration. Since the nature of the business is one-on-one interaction, the trainer must be well prepared and completely locked-in while they are with the client.

Museum Educator: As the name suggests, my job as a museum educator is an amalgam of activities. I work at the South Street Seaport Museum, which is located in a historic district in lower Manhattan. The museum is designed to trace the history of the Port of New York through its galleries and exhibits, living history programs, programs and events, educational programs for children and adults, and the largest privately owned collection of historic vessels anywhere in the United States. My job is to bring the past to life and use the elements of the present.

Middle School Counselor: There is never a dull moment—although paperwork is my least favorite part of the job. A typical day involves meeting with students, teachers, and parents to help students focus on doing the best they can in school.

Education Director: My job is to introduce nature and ecology to people young and old aboard the 100-foot Hudson River sloop *Clearwater*. The Hudson River Sloop is a nonprofit organization that was created to defend and restore the Hudson River through research, education, and other activities.

Educational Consultant: I teach classes to teachers about multicultural education and gender equity. I show them how important it is to understand the culture of their students and how that affects their learning. I teach about the horrible problem of prejudice and discrimination based on race, gender, sexual orientation, immigration status, language, and other issues.

College/Career Advisor: I am a college and career expert. I write books, speak, and write a column on college and career advice. I love working with students to help them discover their true gifts and talents. I don't love the detail work, but I have learned to be disciplined about it. It is important to do the things you don't love as well as the things you do enjoy.

Art Teacher: I am an art teacher in a male juvenile correctional facility. The "aha" moment is the aspect of my job that I enjoy the most. Seeing a child understand a concept or idea and be successful in completing an assignment is worth all the hours of hard work. I don't like the mountains of paperwork. And I don't like the fact that many students are released back into their communities without adequate support services.

Librarian: The first thing I want to say is that the stereotype of librarians is not true. I know no librarian who wears a bun, out-of-date glasses, no make-up and sensible shoes and who spends her time saying "shush." With that out of the way, I will say that librarians don't make much money, but they have a very high level of job satisfaction, and that is true for me. I work only part time but I do a very wide variety of things.

I work in a public library in the children's department, and a lot of my work is with teens. In addition to being responsible for our teen collections of books, magazines, music, etc., I co-run our teen advisory board, and plan lots of teen programs, like a summer volunteer program, summer reading club, and events like mendhi workshops and a pizza taste-off. With other librarians, I do assemblies in our city's middle schools twice a year, telling kids about our programs and some great books we think they might like to read.

In addition to working with the teens I write bibliographies and graded booklists, so reading a lot and keeping up with new books is a necessary (and really enjoyable) part of the job. I also work with groups of schoolchildren who come to the library on field trips. The teachers select what we do with the kids. Most often this is a tour of the library and a storytime for younger kids, and some kind of a reference lesson for older kids (i.e. using electronic databases or the Internet). On occasion, I tell stories from memory to the younger kids, sometimes using props like stuffed animals or a flannel board.

Success Lesson #2:
Career goals change and so do you.

- **When you were in high school, what career did you hope to pursue?**

    Nursery School Teacher: I had no idea but I knew I wanted to work with people.

    Speech-Language Pathologist: I've always wanted to be a speech-language therapist.

    Teacher of the Visually Impaired: I wanted to be an artist.

    Director of Library Services: Librarian was always it for me.

    Personal Trainer/Nutritionist: A doctor.

    Museum Educator: An architect.

    Middle School Counselor: Corporate executive

    Education Director: Ecologist or paleontologist were careers that interested me.

    Educational Consultant: It was a toss-up between teacher and doctor.

    College/Career Advisor: I didn't have a clue what I wanted to do. I briefly considered nursing.

    Art Teacher: When I was a teenager, I wasn't even aware that places like where I work existed. My vision as a teen was to be a commercial artist.

- **What was it that made you change directions?**

    Librarian: Getting to know myself better as an adult. Choosing a career that really fit my interests and abilities.

    Teacher of the Visually Impaired: Volunteer work.

    Museum Educator: When I returned to New York City after being away for twenty years, I became more interested in historic preservation, and this was an easy fit with the mission of this particular museum.

    Middle School Counselor: Ten years in commercial banking, as a lending officer, convinced me my unique potential was not best utilized in a corporate environment. I started to substitute teach and found a love for working with students.

Success Lesson #3:
One things leads to another along any career path.

- ## How did you end up doing what you're doing now?

Nursery School Teacher: I became a social worker first, then a teacher because it fit into my schedule as a mom.

Director of Library Services: In eighth grade, having volunteered for two years in the junior high library and being impressed with the librarian, I decided I wanted to be a librarian.

Personal Trainer/Nutritionist: What kept me moving toward my goal was my own sense of determination and persistence.

Museum Educator: I was working in book publishing when I discovered the South Street Seaport. My time was my own and I was casting about for something more interesting to do. One day I went with my mother on a cruise on a sloop which left from the museum pier. The museum was distributing fliers, part of which was a solicitation for volunteers. I first became a docent and when a position opened in the education department I became full-time staff.

Education Director: I've always had an intense love of nature. The natural world has always been a refuge and a source of inspiration.

Educational Consultant: I wanted to be in a helping profession that involved helping people learn while at the same time helping people with emotional and social issues.

Success Lesson #4:
There's more than one way to get an education.

- **Where did you learn the skills of your field, both formally (school) and informally (experience)?**

   Teacher of the Visually Impaired: Going to a university program that specifically certifies teachers of the visually impaired was how I prepared myself for this work.

   Personal Trainer/Nutritionist: My formal college education is not what prepared me best for my current occupation. Much of what I have learned about exercise physiology and training came from being in the gym environment so often. I would latch onto individuals that I would meet at gyms who seemed like they knew what they were doing. I would ask questions and experiment. The rest I learned by picking up the books and studying independently.

   Museum Educator: My education in both architecture and psychology (for teaching skills) was most helpful. To work in a museum, having an area of expert knowledge is very important. This can be developed on the job or brought to the institution as one's unique contribution.

   Middle School Counselor: Earning a master's degree in school counseling and on-site internships were part of my formal education. The desire to help other people and an unconditional positive regard for each student are two key personal attributes that helped me.

Education Director: My college degree in biology helped, but my life experience and trial-and-error experience of teaching has been the most important.

Art Teacher: Curiosity and risk taking are at the top of my list! Sometimes I feel like an annoying two year old, but my favorite questions are "why" and "what if."

Educational Consultant: Certainly being a teacher for over 25 years has given me great opportunities to learn and grow. I have read and studied much in the area of psychology and good teaching practices. I have studied a lot about the civil rights movement and the injustices people have suffered. I try to learn as much about the law as possible in order to help people stand up for themselves.

College/Career Advisor: I wrote my first book when I was 25. I had an instinct about what the book should be about and I stayed true to that instinct even though I didn't have an MBA, a Ph.D., or any other credentials to my name. Sometimes a good idea is a good idea. You have to believe in it.

Success Lesson #5:
Good choices and hard work are a potent combination.

- **What are you most proud of in your career?**

Teacher of the Visually Impaired: Seeing children graduate from high school that I worked with when they were toddlers, who I taught to read, and have seen grow and mature into young adults.

Personal Trainer/Nutritionist: My most important accomplishment has been the establishment of a fitness and nutrition program for cancer survivors.

Education Director: I'm very proud that every year, 14,000 people experience the Hudson River aboard the sloop Clearwater. It's an amazing place to learn.

Educational Consultant: I have had the ability to positively influence hundreds (possibly thousands) of teachers to become better teachers through my workshops, lectures, and the conferences I run. I also help students, teachers, and parents understand their civil rights and have helped many people successfully use the law to fight for justice.

College/Career Advisor: I have been asked to be a keynote speaker at several national learning conferences. I enjoy working with educators to help them to be more effective with the teen audience.

Success Lesson #6:
You can learn from other people's mistakes.

- **Is there anything you wish you had done differently?**

    Speech-Language Pathologist: Oh, I suppose I should have known better, at times, when, where, and with whom to express my opinions and beliefs for the benefit of students! But then again, controversy was sometimes the launching pad for some of my more creative positions!

    Personal Trainer/Nutritionist: Yes, I wish I had decided upon my career earlier in life and stuck with it (whether it be medicine or training). I think I would be much further along in my career if I had done so.

    Middle School Counselor: I think each experience I had was important in bringing me to where I am today. I would have liked to have more of my own children or perhaps adopted a child.

    Education Director: I sometimes wish that I had gone back to school for an advanced degree earlier in life, but then again I don't regret any of the experiences my choices allowed.

    Educational Consultant: I wish I had traveled more to see others parts of the country and world before I settled where I am now. The culture and politics and social climate of where you live are so important. You should try to find a good match.

    College/Career Advisor: I wish I had been more balanced. I did so many career things early on that I didn't start a family. Now, I may be one of the oldest moms on the planet.

    Art Teacher: Nope. The older I get, the more I appreciate the fact that each of us is unique and our uniqueness is a result of a synthesis of all our life experiences.

Success Lesson #7:
A little advice goes a long way.

- **What advice do you have for a young person just getting started?**

    Nursery School Teacher: Go for your dreams—you never know where they might lead.

    Director of Library Services: Learn from both good and bad work experiences.

Museum Educator: Cultivate your interests and learn the most you can about whatever particularly interests you. This will become the base of strength for developing your skills.

Education Director: My first advice is to learn a language other than English if you haven't already. That will serve you in ways you cannot imagine.

Educational Consultant: Talk to your teachers about what teaching is like. Help out in classes. Volunteer to teach swimming, first aid, and summer camps to get experience. Get life experiences—travel, see the country, try different kinds of jobs—before you decide.

College/Career Advisor: Figure out your own passions and talents. You can't help others do that if you haven't done your own personal work.

Librarian: Spend some time in libraries. You can be a volunteer while you are in middle or high school, and teens over the age of 14 can work in public libraries as a page, shelving books. If you think you'd like to work with books or information, but aren't sure public libraries are right for you, visit some other libraries and speak to the librarians in those positions (call first). There are libraries in hospitals, corporations, law firms, and universities. Some librarians work primarily with computerized resources, others with more of a variety of print and electronic materials.

If there is a master's in library science program at a college or university where you live, get a copy of the catalog or visit. Get some idea of the kind of courses that are required, and what kind of preparation you'll need. While an undergraduate degree is required, there is no required major. People enter library school with degrees in everything from English literature to anthropology (mine). In fact, many people in library school have advanced degrees in other subjects, even law degrees and Ph.Ds. It's a very diverse field.

Big Activity #7:
who knows what you need to know?

It's one thing to read about conducting an informational interview, but it's another thing altogether to actually do one. Now it's your turn to shine. Just follow these steps for doing it like a pro!

Step 1: Identify the people you want to talk to about their work.

Step 2: Set up a convenient time to meet in person or talk over the phone.

Step 3: Make up a list of questions that reflect things you'd really like to know about that person's work. Go for the open questions you just read about.

Step 4: Talk away! Take notes as your interviewee responds to each question.

Step 5: Use your notes to write up a "news" article that describes the person and his or her work.

Step 6: Place all your notes and the finished "news" article in your Big Question AnswerBook.

Big Activity #7: **who knows what you need to know?**

contact information	appointments/sample questions
name	day time
company	location
title	
address	
	sample questions:
phone	
email	
name	day time
company	location
title	
address	
	sample questions:
phone	
email	
name	day time
company	location
title	
address	
	sample questions:
phone	
email	

Big Activity #7: **who knows what you need to know?**

questions	answers

INTERVIEW NOTES

Big Activity #7: **who knows what you need to know?**

questions	answers

INTERVIEW NOTES

Big Activity #7: **who knows what you need to know?**

NEWS

Big Activity #7: **who knows what you need to know?**

NEWS

Big Question #8:
how can you find out what a career is really like?

There are some things you just have to figure out for yourself. Things like whether your interest in pursuing a career in marine biology is practical if you plan to live near the Mojave Desert.

Other things you have to see for yourself. Words are sometimes not enough when it comes to conveying what a job is really like on a day-to-day basis—what it looks like, sounds like, and feels like.

Here are a few ideas for conducting an on-the-job reality check.

identify typical types of workplaces

Think of all the places that jobs like the ones you like take place. Almost all of the careers in this book, or ones very similar to them, exist in the corporate world, in the public sector, and in the military. And don't forget the option of going into business for yourself!

For example: Are you interested in public relations? You can find a place for yourself in almost any sector of our economy. Of course, companies definitely want to promote their products. But don't limit yourself to the Fortune 500 corporate world. Hospitals, schools, and manufacturers need your services. Cities, states, and even countries also need your services. They want to increase tourism, get businesses to relocate there, and convince workers to live there or students to study there. Each military branch needs to recruit new members and to show how they are using the money they receive from the government for medical research, taking care of families, and other non-news-breaking uses. Charities, community organizations, and even religious groups want to promote the good things they are doing so that they will get more members, volunteers, contributions, and funding. Political candidates, parties, and special interest groups all want to promote their messages. Even actors, dancers, and writers need to promote themselves.

Not interested in public relations but know you want a career that involves lots of writing? You've thought about becoming the more obvious choices—novelist, newspaper reporter, or English teacher. But you don't want to overlook other interesting possibilities, do you?

What if you also enjoy technical challenges? Someone has to write the documentation for all those computer games and software.

Love cars? Someone has to write those owner's manuals too.

Ditto on those government reports about safety and environmental standards for industries.

Maybe community service is your thing. You can mix your love for helping people with writing grant proposals seeking funds for programs at hospitals, day care centers, or rehab centers.

Talented in art and design? Those graphics you see in magazine advertisements, on your shampoo bottle, and on a box of cereal all have to be created by someone.

That someone could be you.

find out about the job outlook

Organizations like the U.S. Bureau of Labor Statistics spend a lot of time and energy gathering data on what kinds of jobs are most in demand now and what kinds are projected to be in demand in the future. Find out what the job outlook is for a career you like. A good resource for this data can be found on-line at America's Career InfoNet at *www.acinet.org/acinet*.

This information will help you understand whether the career options you find most appealing are viable. In other words, job outlook data will give you a better sense of your chances of actually finding gainful employment in your chosen profession—a rather important consideration from any standpoint.

Be realistic. You may really, really want to be a film critic at a major newspaper. Maybe your ambition is to become the next Roger Ebert.

Think about this. How many major newspapers are there? Is it reasonable to pin all your career hopes on a job for which there are only about 10 positions in the whole country? That doesn't mean that it's impossible to achieve your ambition. After all, someone has to fill those positions. It should just temper your plans with realism and perhaps encourage you to have a back-up plan, just in case.

look at training requirements

Understand what it takes to prepare yourself for a specific job. Some jobs require only a high school diploma. Others require a couple of years of technical training, while still others require four years or more in college.

Be sure to investigate a variety of training options. Look at training programs and colleges you may like to attend. Check out their websites to see what courses are required for the major you want. Make sure you're willing to "do the time" in school to prepare yourself for a particular occupation.

see for yourself

There's nothing quite like seeing for yourself what a job is like. Talk with a teacher or guidance counselor to arrange a job-shadowing opportunity with someone who is in the job or in a similar one.

Job shadowing is an activity that involves actually spending time at work with someone to see what a particular job is like up close and personal. It's an increasingly popular option and your school may participate in specially designated job-shadowing days. For some especially informative resources on job shadowing, visit *www.jobshadow.org*.

Another way to test-drive different careers is to find summer jobs and internships that are similar to the career you hope to pursue.

make a Plan B

Think of the alternatives! Often it's not possible to have a full-time job in the field you love. Some jobs just don't pay enough to meet the needs of every person or family. Maybe you recognize that you don't have the talent, drive, or commitment to rise to the top. Or, perhaps you can't afford the years of work it takes to get established or you place a higher priority on spending time with family than that career might allow.

If you can see yourself in any of those categories, DO NOT GIVE UP on what you love! There is always more than one way to live out your dreams. Look at some of the other possibilities in this book. Find a way to integrate your passion into other jobs or your free time.

Lots of people manage to accomplish this in some fairly impressive ways. For instance, the Knicks City Dancers, known for their incredible performances and for pumping up the crowd at Knicks basketball games, include an environmental engineer, a TV news assignment editor, and a premed student, in addition to professional dancers. The Broadband Pickers, a North Texas bluegrass band, is made up of five lawyers and one businessman. In fact, even people who are extremely successful in a field that they love find ways to indulge their other passions. Paul Newman, the actor and director, not only drives race cars as a hobby, but also produces a line of gourmet foods and donates the profits to charity.

Get the picture? Good. Hang in there and keep moving forward in your quest to find your way toward a great future.

Big Activity #8:
how can you find out
what a career is really like?

This activity will help you conduct a reality check about your future career in two ways. First, it prompts you to find out more about the nitty-gritty details you really need to know to make a well-informed career choice. Second, it helps you identify strategies for getting a firsthand look at what it's like to work in a given profession—day in and day out.

Here's how to get started:

Step 1: Write the name of the career you're considering at the top of a sheet of paper (or use the following worksheets if this is your book).

Step 2: Create a checklist (or, if this is your book, use the one provided on the following pages) covering two types of reality-check items.

First, list four types of information to investigate:
● training requirements
● typical workplaces
● job outlook
● similar occupations

Second, list three types of opportunities to pursue:
● job shadowing
● apprenticeship
● internship

Step 3: Use resources such as America's Career InfoNet at *www.acinet.org* and Career OneStop at *www.careeronestop.org* to seek out the information you need.

Step 4: Make an appointment with your school guidance counselor to discuss how to pursue hands-on opportunities to learn more about this occupation. Use the space provided on the following worksheets to jot down preliminary contact information and a brief summary of why or why not each career is right for you.

Step 5: When you're finished, place these notes in your Big Question AnswerBook.

Big Activity #8: **how can you find out
what a career is really like?**

career choice:	
training requirements	
typical workplaces	
job outlook	
similar occupations	

INFORMATION

Big Activity #8: **how can you find out what a career is really like?**

job shadowing	when: where: who: observations and impressions:
apprenticeship	when: where: who: observations and impressions:
internship	when: where: who: observations and impressions:

OPPORTUNITIES

Big Question #9:
how do you know when you've made the right choice?

When it comes right down to it, finding the career that's right for you is like shopping in a mall with 12,000 different stores. Finding the right fit may require trying on lots of different options.

All the Big Questions you've answered so far have been designed to expand your career horizons and help you clarify what you really want in a career. The next step is to see how well you've managed to integrate your interests, capabilities, goals, and ambitions with the realities of specific opportunities.

There are two things for you to keep in mind as you do this.

First, recognize the value of all the hard work you did to get to this point. If you've already completed the first eight activities thoughtfully and honestly, whatever choices you make will be based on solid knowledge about yourself and your options. You've learned to use a process that works just as well now, when you're trying to get an inkling of what you want to do with your life, as it will later when you have solid job offers on the table and need to make decisions that will affect your life and family.

Second, always remember that sometimes, even when you do everything right, things don't turn out the way you'd planned. That's called life. It happens. And it's not the end of the world. Even if you make what seems to be a bad choice, know this—there's no such thing as a wasted experience. The paths you take, the training you receive, the people you meet—they ultimately fall together like puzzle pieces to make you who you are and prepare you for what you're meant to do.

That said, here's a strategy to help you confirm that you are making the very best choices you can.

Big Activity #9:
how do you know when you've made the right choice?

One way to confirm that the choices you are making are right for you is to look at both sides of this proverbial coin: what you are looking for and what each career offers. The following activity will help you think this through.

Step 1: To get started, make two charts with four columns (or, if this is your book, use the following worksheets).

Step 2: Label the first column of the first chart as "Yes Please!" Under this heading list all the qualities you absolutely must have in a future job. This might include factors such as the kind of training you'd prefer to pursue (college, apprenticeship, etc.); the type of place where you'd like to work (big office, high-tech lab, in the great outdoors, etc.); and the sorts of people you want to work with (children, adults, people with certain needs, etc.). It may also include salary requirements or dress code preferences.

Step 3: Now at the top of the next three columns write the names of three careers you are considering. (This is a little like Big Activity #3 where you examined your work values. But now you know a lot more and you're ready to zero in on specific careers.)

Step 4: Go down the list and use an *X* to indicate careers that do indeed feature the desired preferences. Use an *O* to indicate those that do not.

Step 5: Tally up the number of *Xs* and *Os* at the bottom of each career column to find out which comes closest to your ideal job.

Step 6: In the first column of the second chart add a heading called "No Thanks!" This is where you'll record the factors you simply prefer not to deal with. Maybe long hours, physically demanding work, or jobs that require years of advanced training just don't cut it for you. Remember that part of figuring out what you do want to do involves understanding what you don't want to do.

Step 7: Repeat steps 2 through 5 for these avoid-at-all-costs preferences as you did for the must-have preferences above.

Big Activity #9: **how do you know when you've made the right choice?**

yes please!	career #1	career #2	career #3
totals	__X__O	__X__O	__X__O

Big Activity #9: **how do you know when you've made the right choice?**

no thanks!	career #1	career #2	career #3
totals	__X__O	__X__O	__X__O

? Big Question #10:
what's next?

Think of this experience as time well invested in your future. And expect it to pay off in a big way down the road. By now, you have worked (and perhaps wrestled) your way through nine important questions:

- ? Big Question #1: **who are you?**
- ? Big Question #2: **what are your interests and strengths?**
- ? Big Question #3: **what are your work values?**
- ? Big Question #4: **what is your work personality?**
- ? Big Question #5: **do you have the right skills?**
- ? Big Question #6: **are you on the right path?**
- ? Big Question #7: **who knows what you need to know?**
- ? Big Question #8: **how can you find out what a career is really like?**
- ? Big Question #9: **how do you know when you've made the right choice?**

But what if you still don't have a clue about what you want to do with your life?

Don't worry. You're talking about one of the biggest life decisions you'll ever make. These things take time.

It's okay if you don't have all the definitive answers yet. At least you do know how to go about finding them. The process you've used to work through this book is one that you can rely on throughout your life to help you sort through the options and make sound career decisions.

So what's next?

More discoveries, more exploration, and more experimenting with success are what come next. Keep at it and you're sure to find your way to wherever your dreams and ambitions lead you.

And, just for good measure, here's one more Big Activity to help point you in the right direction.

what's next?

List five things you can do to move forward in your career planning process (use a separate sheet if you need to). Your list may include tasks such as talking to your guidance counselor about resources your school makes available, checking out colleges or other types of training programs that can prepare you for your life's work, or finding out about job-shadowing or internship opportunities in your community. Remember to include any appropriate suggestions from the Get Started Now! list included with each career profile in Section 2 of this book.

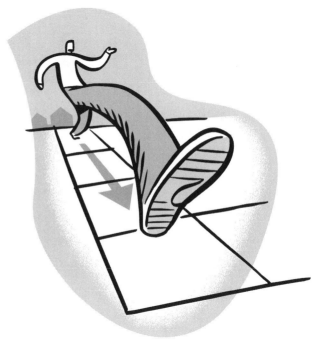

Big Activity #10: **what's next?**

career planning to-do list

1

2

3

4

5

a final word

You are now officially equipped with the tools you need to track down a personally appropriate profession any time you have the need or desire. You've discovered more about who you are and what you want. You've explored a variety of career options within a very important industry. You've even taken it upon yourself to experiment with what it might be like to actually work in certain occupations.

Now it's up to you to put all this newfound knowledge to work for you. While you're at it, here's one more thing to keep in mind: Always remember that there's no such thing as a wasted experience. Certainly some experiences are more positive than others, but they all teach us something.

Chances are you may not get everything right the first time out. It may turn out that you were incorrect about how much you would love to go to a certain college or pursue a particular profession. That doesn't mean you're doomed to failure. It simply means that you've lived and learned. Sometimes you just won't know for sure about one direction or another until you try things out a bit. Nothing about your future has to be written in stone. Allow yourself some freedom to experiment with various options until you find something that really clicks for you.

Figuring out what you want to do with the rest of your life is a big deal. It's probably one of the most exciting and among the most intimidating decisions you'll ever make. It's a decision that warrants clear-headed thought and wholehearted investigation. It's a process that's likely to take you places you never dared imagine if you open yourself up to all the possibilities. Take a chance on yourself and seek out and follow your most valued hopes and dreams into the workplace.

Best wishes for a bright future!

Appendix

a virtual support team

As you continue your quest to determine just what it is you want to do with your life, you'll find that you are not alone. There are many people and organizations who want to help you succeed. Here are two words of advice—let them! Take advantage of all the wonderful resources so readily available to you.

The first place to start is your school's guidance center. There you are quite likely to find a variety of free resources which include information about careers, colleges, and other types of training opportunities; details about interesting events, job shadowing activities, and internship options; and access to useful career assessment tools.

In addition, since you are the very first generation on the face of the earth to have access to a world of information just the click of a mouse away—use it! The following Internet resources provide all kinds of information and ideas that can help you find your future.

make an informed choice

Following are five of the very best career-oriented websites currently on-line. Be sure to bookmark these websites and visit them often as you consider various career options.

America's Career InfoNet *www.acinet.org/acinet/default.asp*

Quite possibly the most comprehensive source of career exploration anywhere, this U.S. Department of Labor website includes all kinds of current information about wages, market conditions, employers, and employment trends. Make sure to visit the site's career video library where you'll find links to over 450 videos featuring real people doing real jobs.

Careers & Colleges *www.careersandcolleges.com*

Each year Careers & Colleges publishes four editions of *Careers & Colleges* magazine, designed to help high school students set and meet their academic, career, and financial goals. Ask your guidance counselor about receiving free copies. You'll also want to visit the excellent Careers and Colleges website. Here you'll encounter their "Virtual Guidance Counselor," an interactive career database that allows you to match your interests with college majors or careers that are right for you.

Career Voyages *www.careervoyages.gov*

This website is brought to you compliments of collaboration between the U.S. Department of Labor and the U.S. Department of Education and is designed especially for students like you. Here you'll find information on high-growth, high-demand occupations and the skills and education needed to attain those jobs.

Job Shadow *www.jobshadow.org*

See your future via a variety of on-line virtual job-shadowing videos and interviews featuring people with fascinating jobs.

My Cool Career *www.mycoolcareer.com*

This website touts itself as the "coolest career dream site for teens and 20's." See for yourself as you work your way through a variety of useful self-assessment quizzes, listen to an assortment of on-line career shows, and explore all kinds of career resources.

investigate local opportunities

To get a better understanding of employment happenings in your state, visit these state-specific career information websites.

Alabama
www.ajb.org/al
www.al.plusjobs.com

Alaska
www.jobs.state.ak.us
www.akcis.org/default.htm

Arizona
www.ajb.org/az
www.ade.state.az.us/cte/AZCrn
* project10.asp*

Arkansas
www.ajb.org/ar
www.careerwatch.org
www.ioscar.org/ar

California
www.calmis.ca.gov
www.ajb.org/ca
www.eurekanet.org

Colorado
www.coloradocareer.net
www.coworkforce.com/lmi

Connecticut
www1.ctdol.state.ct.us/jcc
www.ctdol.state.ct.us/lmi

Delaware
www.ajb.org/de
www.delewareworks.com

District of Columbia
www.ajb.org/dc
www.dcnetworks.org

Florida
www.Florida.access.bridges.com
www.employflorida.net

Georgia
www.gcic.peachnet.edu
  (Ask your school guidance counselor
  for your school's free password and
  access code)
www.dol.state.ga.us/js

Hawaii
www.ajb.org/hi
www.careerkokua.org

Idaho
www.ajb.org/id
www.cis.idaho.gov

Illinois
www.ajb.org/il
www.ilworkinfo.com

Indiana
www.ajb.org/in
http://icpac.indiana.edu

Iowa
www.ajb.org/ia
www.state.ia.us/iccor

Kansas
www.ajb.org/ks
www.kansasjoblink.com/ada

Kentucky
www.ajb.org/ky

Louisiana
www.ajb.org/la
www.ldol.state.la.us/jobpage.asp

Maine
www.ajb.org/me
www.maine.gov/labor/lmis

Maryland
www.ajb.org/md
www.careernet.state.md.us

Massachusetts
www.ajb.org/ma
http://masscis.intocareers.org

Michigan
www.mois.org

Minnesota
www.ajb.org/mn
www.iseek.org

Mississippi
www.ajb.org/ms
www.mscareernet.org

Missouri
www.ajb.org/mo
www.greathires.org

Montana
www.ajb.org/mt
http://jsd.dli.state.mt.us/mjshome.asp

Nebraska
www.ajb.org/ne
www.careerlink.org

New Hampshire
www.nhes.state.nh.us

New Jersey
www.ajb.org/nj
www.wnjpin.net/coei

New Mexico
www.ajb.org/nm
www.dol.state.nm.us/soicc/upto21.html

Nevada
www.ajb.org/nv
http://nvcis.intocareers.org

New York
www.ajb.org/ny
www.nycareerzone.org

North Carolina
www.ajb.org/nc
www.ncsoicc.org
www.nccareers.org

North Dakota
www.ajb.org/nd
www.imaginend.com
www.ndcrn.com/students

Ohio
www.ajb.org/oh
https://scoti.ohio.gov/scoti_lexs

Oklahoma
www.ajb.org/ok
www.okcareertech.org/guidance
http://okcrn.org

Oregon
www.hsd.k12.or.us/crls

Pennsylvania
www.ajb.org/pa
www.pacareerlink.state.pa.us

Rhode Island
www.ajb.org/ri
www.dlt.ri.gov/lmi/jobseeker.htm

South Carolina
www.ajb.org/sc
www.scois.org/students.htm

South Dakota
www.ajb.org/sd

Tennessee
www.ajb.org/tn
www.tcids.utk.edu

Texas
www.ajb.org/tx
www.ioscar.org/tx
www.cdr.state.tx.us/Hotline/Hotline.html

Utah
www.ajb.org/ut
http://jobs.utah.gov/wi/occi.asp

Vermont
www.ajb.org/vt
www.vermontjoblink.com
www.vtlmi.info/oic.cfm

Virginia
www.ajb.org/va
www.vacrn.net

Washington
www.ajb.org/wa
www.workforceexplorer.com
www.wa.gov/esd/lmea/soicc/
  sohome.htm

West Virginia
www.ajb.org/wv
www.state.wv.us/bep/lmi

Wisconsin
www.ajb.org/wi
www.careers4wi.wisc.edu
http://wiscareers.wisc.edu/splash.asp

Wyoming
www.ajb.org/wy
http://uwadmnweb.uwyo.edu/SEO/
  wcis.htm

get a job

Whether you're curious about the kinds of jobs currently in big demand or you're actually looking for a job, the following websites are a great place to do some virtual job-hunting.

America's Job Bank www.ajb.org

Another example of your (or, more accurately, your parent's) tax dollars at work, this well-organized website is sponsored by the U.S. Department of Labor. Job seekers can post resumes and use the site's search engines to search through over a million job listings by location or by job type.

Monster.com www.monster.com

One of the Internet's most widely used employment websites, this is where you can search for specific types of jobs in specific parts of the country, network with millions of people, and find useful career advice.

explore by special interests

An especially effective way to explore career options is to look at careers associated with a personal interest or fascination with a certain type of industry. The following websites help you narrow down your options in a focused way.

What Interests You? *www.bls.gov/k12*

This Bureau of Labor Statistics website provides information about careers associated with 12 special interest areas: math, reading, science, social studies, music and arts, building and fixing things, helping people, computers, law, managing money, sports, and nature.

Construct My Future *www.constructmyfuture.com*

With over $600 billion annually devoted to new construction projects, about 6 million Americans build careers in this industry. This website, sponsored by the Association of Equipment Distributors, the Association of Equipment Manufacturers, and Associated General Contractors, introduces an interesting array of construction-related professions.

Dream It Do It *www.dreamit-doit.com*

In order to make manufacturing a preferred career choice by 2010, the National Association of Manufacturing's Center for Workforce Success is reaching out to young adults and, their parents, educators, communities, and policy-makers to change their minds about manufacturing's future and its careers. This website introduces high-demand 21st-century manufacturing professions many will find surprising and worthy of serious consideration.

Get Tech *www.gettech.org*

Another award-winning website from the National Association of Manufacturing.

Take Another Look *www.Nrf.com/content/foundation/rcp/main.htm*

The National Retail Federation challenges students to take another look at their industry by introducing a wide variety of careers associated with marketing and advertising, store management, sales, distribution and logistics, e-commerce, and more.

Index

Page numbers in **boldface** indicate main articles. Page numbers in *italics* indicate photographs.

National Association for Sport & Physical Education (NASPE) 90

National Association for the Education of Young Children 93

National Association of Agricultural Educators 53

National Association of County Agricultural Agents 53

National Association of Elementary School Principals 96

National Association of Financial Aid Administrators 121

National Association of Manufacturers 43, 176

National Association of School Nurses 103

National Association of School Psychologists (NASP) 105

National Association of Secondary School Principals 96

National Association of Social Workers (NASW) 107

National Association of State Foresters 71

National Association of Student Personnel Administrators 121

National Career Development Association 44

National Center for ESL Literacy Education (NCLE) 67

National Centers for Career and Technical Education 41

National Clearinghouse for Paraeducator Resources 88

National Clearinghouse for Professions in Special Education (NCPSE) 106, 115

National Collegiate Athletic Association (NCAA) 47

National Conference of Teachers of English (NCTE) 110

National Council of Teachers of Mathematics 110

National Education Association 64, 110

National Federation of the Blind 126

National High School Coaches Association 47

National Information Center for Children and Youth with Disabilities (NICHCY) 115

National Institute for Correctional Education 58

National Network for Child Care 94

National Orientation Counselors Association 122

National Resource Center for Paraprofessionals 88

National Retail Foundation 176

National Science Teachers Association (NSTA) 110

National Strength and Conditioning Association (NSCA) 72

National Student Speech Language Hearing Association (NSSLHA) 38

National Stuttering Association (NSA) 118

National Teachers Recruitment Clearinghouse 64, 88, 110

National Trust for Historic Preservation 85

Natural Wonders: A Guide to Early Childhood for Environmental Educators 69

NCAA. *See* National Collegiate Athletic Association

NCLE. *See* National Center for ESL Literacy Education

NCPSE. *See* National Clearinghouse for Professions in Special Education

NCTE. *See* National Conference of Teachers of English

NetResults 121

New Jersey v. T.L.O. 62

new phys ed 90–92

New Teachers 64

New York, New York 85, 143, 144, 146

Newman, Paul 160

NICHCY. *See* National Information Center for Children and Youth with Disabilities

North American Association for Environmental Education 69

NSA. *See* National Stuttering Association

NSCA. *See* National Strength and Conditioning Association

NSSLHA. *See* National Student Speech Language Hearing Association

NSTA. *See* National Science Teachers Association

nursery school teacher
    interview 143, 146, 147, 150

nutritionist 132

O

O*Net 17, 18, 45

Occupational Outlook Handbook 45

occupational therapist 132

Ogaz, Nancy 116

Ohio Lions Club Eye Research (website) 126

open questions 141

Orientation and Mobility in the Public Schools (Web page) 126

orientation and mobility specialist. *See* teacher of the visually impaired

P

Palo Alto, California 143

paraprofessional 30, 33, **88–89**

PBS Teacher Source (website) 79

PE 4 Life (website) 90

PE Central (website) 90
    Job Center 90

Peace Corps 100

Pearl Harbor 85

personal trainer/nutritionist
    interview 143–144, 146–150

personnel administrator 132

Phi Delta Kappa 64, 110

Philadelphia Museum of Art 60

Philbrick Rodman 116

Physical Education for Progress Act 92

physical education teacher 30, 33, **90–92**

PLA. *See* Public Library Association

Plymouth, Massachusetts 85

Plymouth Plantation 85

Poughkeepsie, New York 143

preschool teacher 30, **93–95**

principal 30, 34, **96–97**